# INSIDE THE
# LEADER'S
# HEAD

# INSIDE THE LEADER'S HEAD

Unraveling Personal Obstacles to Ministry

**VIRGINIA TODD HOLEMAN**
**STEPHEN L. MARTYN**

Abingdon Press
*Nashville*

INSIDE THE LEADER'S HEAD
UNRAVELING PERSONAL OBSTACLES TO MINISTRY

### Library of Congress Cataloging-in-Publication Data

Holeman, Virginia Todd, 1953-
  Inside the leader's head : unraveling personal obstacles to ministry / Virginia Todd Holeman and Stephen L. Martyn.
    p. cm.
  Includes bibliographical references and index.
  ISBN 978-0-687-64728-6 (binding: adhesive - lay- flat : alk. paper)
  1. Christian leadership. 2. Clergy—Psychology. I. Martyn, Stephen L. II. Title.

BV652.1.H66 2008
253'.2—dc22

2008005463

Scripture, unless noted otherwise, is from the New Revised Standard Version of the Bible, copyright 1989, Division of Christian Education of the National Council of the Churches of Christ in the United States of America. Used by permission. All rights reserved.

Scripture marked NIV is taken from the Holy Bible, NEW INTERNATIONAL VERSION®. Copyright © 1973, 1978, 1984 by International Bible Society. All rights reserved throughout the world. Used by permission of International Bible Society.

Scripture marked KJV is from the King James or Authorized Version of the Bible.

Scripture marked TNIV is taken from the Holy Bible, TODAY'S NEW INTERNATIONAL VERSION®. Copyright © 2001, 2005 International Bible Society. All rights reserved throughout the world. Used by permission of the International Bible Society.

Prayer on page 47 is from A Service of Word and Table II © 1972, 1980, 1985, 1989 The United Methodist Publishing House. Used by permission.

List on pages 71–73 is from *Extraordinary Relationships: A New Way of Thinking about Human Interactions* by R. M. Gilbert. Copyright © 1992. Reprinted with permission of John Wiley & Sons, Inc.

08 09 10 11 12 13 14 15 16 17—10 9 8 7 6 5 4 3 2 1
MANUFACTURED IN THE UNITED STATES OF AMERICA

This work I write in loving memory of my parents, the Reverend Benjamin C. and Virginia P. Holeman, who were my first examples of Christlike church leaders. –V. T. H.

To my parents, who raised me in the church, who demonstrated servant leadership to me, and who have been my best cheerleaders. —S. L. M.

# CONTENTS

# PREFACE

We (Toddy and Steve) bring our own unique gifts and perspectives to this endeavor. And they shape how we think about church leadership. Toddy grew up as a preacher's kid and has been an active laywoman throughout her life. She is a member of The Wesleyan Church. Professionally, she not only teaches at Asbury Seminary, she is also a licensed marriage and family therapist and delights in bringing these insights about how relationships work to her teaching as a seminary professor. In her role as a faculty member, she has also served as a committee chair, a department chair, and an associate dean (not all at the same time!). Steve has been an elder in The United Methodist Church since 1977. He has been the pastor of six congregations. In addition, he served as Director of Spiritual Formation for the Kentucky Annual Conference of The United Methodist Church and now teaches Christian Leadership and Spirituality at Asbury Seminary. Steve brings his wide-ranging background dealing with the practical reality of the pastoral life to this book. We both are grounded in a Wesleyan way of theological thinking, and we bring that lens and love to our discussion as well.

Church leaders include women and men in lay and ordained positions. The leadership issues that we address in this book are not gender specific and we have employed a variety of ways to apply our discussion to both women and men. Sometimes we refer to leaders (plural) and avoid dealing with specific gender entirely. Other times we have used alternating single pronouns (i.e., he or she).

In that church leadership is far more of an art and a discipline than it is a mere profession, we pray that this text will be used by the Holy Spirit to help form God's leaders into women and men of joy who fulfill their high calling in Christ Jesus and who bring transformational blessings into the lives of those they are called to serve.

Toddy and Steve

# CHAPTER ONE

# IT'S NOT ABOUT ME . . . OR IS IT?

*What good will it be for you to gain the whole world, yet forfeit your soul?—Matthew 16:26 TNIV*

The day is filled with joyful anticipation. Friends and family are seated in the large auditorium, eagerly awaiting the entrance of their son or daughter, husband or wife, friend or colleague. In a nearby location students and seminary faculty, bedecked in all the glory of academic regalia, begin the graduation procession. Soon each student is called by name to receive his or her diploma. Many anticipate completing their ordination requirements in the months (or years) ahead. Others, who are not seeking ordination, look forward to serving in the local church as Christian education directors, youth workers, missionaries, pastoral counselors, church administrators, and the like. A lifetime of church leadership lies ahead. What future awaits these men and women who have prepared for full-time ministry? What stories will they tell when we see them again? Will they tell us about the thrill of victory or the agony of defeat? Will they testify to how ministry provided fertile soil for nurturing personal and social holiness for them and for their congregations? Or will it seem as if their souls have shriveled up because they found themselves in a parched and barren land? Will their eyes shine with the joy of full-time Christian service or will they look at us with the dull gaze of the walking wounded?

All church leaders will experience "victory" *and* "defeat" over the course of their ministry. Church leaders include the ordained and the lay, the full-time staff member and the dedicated volunteer, those who serve on the front lines and those who work behind the scenes. In fact, a leader may be considered as "anyone who has someone following her. If anyone looks to you for wisdom, counsel, or direction, then you are a leader. . . . *Anyone* who wrestles with an uncertain future on behalf of others—anyone who uses [his or her] gifts, talents, or skills to influence the direction of others for the greater good—is a leader" (Allender, 2006, p. 25). Hopefully by the proverbial end of the day the blessings of ministry will outnumber its burdens; and the sorrows that often go along with working closely with people will seem light and momentary when compared to the joy of serving God. Unfortunately, this ratio of blessing to burden and cross to joy is not always maintained. For some leaders the afflictions they experience are overwhelming. As a result, we find the path littered with ministry casualties; men and women who began their leadership with high hopes and later abandoned their leadership role. My (Steve) experience bears this out. Out of the thirty-two persons I was ordained with in the late 1970s, less than 50 percent remain in ordained ministry. And sadly, a number of those dear ones who left ministry did so under the weight of moral collapse.

# A Tale of Two Christian Leaders

I (Toddy) graduated with a master's degree in Christian Ministries. My spiritual gifts and personal graces fit hand-in-glove with the educational life of the church. I never felt called to ordained ministry. I wanted to serve God as a well-trained laywoman. Upon graduation, I began to work in a suburban church as their Director of Christian Education and Youth Ministries. I approached this placement with earnest expectations. The senior pastor and I carried the same theological commitments and the same passion to see people come to a deeper relationship with Jesus Christ. My working relationship with him was strong and collegial. We respected each other and our strengths were complementary. The congregation responded well to my leadership. My relationship with this specific senior pastor and this particular congregation seemed to be a match made in heaven.

At the next conference year a new pastor was appointed to this church. This man of God was different from the former pastor, and tension quickly arose between this newly appointed leader and a group of influential parishioners. Me? I felt as if I were caught smack dab in the middle of a guerrilla war. I tried to remain neutral, but I felt my ability to do so was stretched to the limit. I wanted to be faithful in my relationship with this new pastoral colleague, but *not* taking sides was incredibly challenging at times as my relationship with this subgroup of parishioners predated my working relationship with the new pastor. Predictably the church began to splinter into two camps. The education and youth program began to suffer as many of my most dedicated volunteers left this church. I began to lose heart, and fear arose about my own job security. Privately I wondered if I would be asked to leave because of flagging financial resources or if I should resign because of the differences that I had with the appointed pastor.

At the same time my personal life fell apart as a member of my family became seriously ill, creating a domino effect of unexpected—and often unwanted—changes in my home life. My personal and church struggles lasted for three years. I looked for places of relief but found no refuge from the storms at home or at church, the two locations where I normally refueled. There was no balm in Gilead for me. Eventually the energy required to deal with my personal life crises became all consuming. At the end of three years, I no longer had any strength to fight the good fight on two fronts. My conscience prohibited me from seeking respite in behaviors that were counter to my walk with Christ. In other words, drinking, drugs, or other forms of acting out were not in my repertoire. But something had to give. I resigned from my position at the church because I couldn't resign from life. I began attending a church in a different denomination, in a different town, and carefully hid the ministry gifts that I brought with me. If you had spoken with me then, you would have concluded that I was a church leader who had lost my soul.

My recovery was slow in coming. Because I had to do something, I turned to one of the things that I do best—I went back to school. My original intent was to earn a degree in pastoral counseling and psychology, add this to my ministry portfolio, and eventually return to full-time service as a Christian education director. However, in the midst of all this, God reframed my call. What I had thought of as just the addition of another degree was moved by God to the center stage of my life. I discovered new skills that built upon my spiritual gifts. I entered the world of Christian counseling as a licensed professional counselor. Over the course of my professional development as a Christian counselor, I learned about family system theories in general and family of origin therapy in particular. These perspectives helped me understand what I had experienced as a Christian education director in a different way. Perhaps I would have returned to full-time, vocational ministry in a local church if I had known then what I know now. I prefer to think about my ministry story in a different way. Now I am equipped to come alongside present and future church leaders, and by sharing these same insights with them, I can help them stay spiritually, emotionally, and relationally grounded in the midst of intense ministry pressures.

I (Steve) well remember having to face very quickly the realities of living within a pastor's salary. The Lord had blessed Diane and me with our first child in 1977. We were serving a small rural congregation over sixty miles from a major city. The ministry position simply required that I do a huge amount of driving both within the expansive county that I served and back and forth to various hospitals in the area. We soon came to realize that after covering my professional expenses, it was very difficult to make ends meet for the basic requirements of our family. The church was doing all it could to support us financially, but my faith was not great enough to fill the gap between what the church provided and what we thought our expenses required. Anxiety thus crept in the door of my heart. I worried how I would ever be able to send my children to college and how in the world Diane and I would possibly be able to retire. The situation seemed intolerable to me.

From the fear and anxiety that arose out of my concern of not having enough to provide for basic needs, I began moonlighting with three additional part-time jobs. I worked for a funeral home, helped run a community ambulance service, and took vacation time to work on a farm during harvest seasons. Then in addition, I began investing small amounts of money. In fact, I could only invest $50 a month. Soon I was up and about before 6:00 a.m.—not in order to have prayer and devotions but to listen to the Hong Kong gold and silver markets. Within a few years I was astounded to see a surprising amount of success with my investments. But the price to my spiritual life was costly. The young man who had been sent out to shepherd God's church turned his heart, mind, and affections to becoming a millionaire for God.

In his infinite love, God allowed the small fortune I had made to collapse. My gain was reduced to substantial debt. As I approached the fifth anniversary of ministry in that country church, I had come to the clear conclusion that the only thing I wanted was to leave that church. In a failed effort to provide financial security for my family, I had actually ended up placing us in serious fiscal jeopardy. By the spring of 1981, I just did not care about being a pastor any longer.

I did not leave the ministry. Instead the Lord was extremely gracious and merciful to me in those days and moved us to serve a church close to where I had grown up. From the very first Sunday at this new pastorate, I knew that *if* I was going to survive in ministry I had to do things differently. Now, rather than getting up early to check the world markets and spend hours on trading, I got up early for devotions. I began walking up to the church very early in the mornings (walking so that no one would know I was in the building) and once inside I would literally lock myself in the library, and then throw myself into prayer, scriptural study, meditation, reading of devotional classics, and journaling. In addition I began meeting once a week in a small covenant group with two of the members of that congregation. We mostly just prayed for one another and encouraged one another.

Over a course of two years of faithfully entering into daily times of devotion and weekly times of close fellowship and prayer with others, the Lord worked a marvelous process of reformation and transformation in my heart. The fear and anxiety that led to greed and dissipation of life were replaced with dispositions of devotional living and relational strengthening. Like Toddy, out of this a whole new call arose to return to school for formal, in-depth training in formative spirituality. The Lord literally saved me from losing my soul in ministry.

# Naming the Problem

The conflicts represented by our stories are pretty typical: theological differences, staffing issues, membership fallout, and personal crises. The repercussions of these conflicts are also pretty typical: physical, emotional, and spiritual exhaustion, intense anxiety, and confusion. From our stories you can see that both of us have experienced times when our soul for ministry was threatened by *our responses* to ministry stresses and strains. Our stories are similar in that we went through our own variation of personal trial by fire. But our stories also differ. At the time of our crises Toddy was employed by a suburban church as a full-time lay staff member while Steve, an ordained minister, was appointed as the pastor of a small rural church. Our positions factored into our level of stress and the options that we saw before us. We suspect that some readers will identify more with one of our stories than the other. Our stories raise for us the question that forms the heart of this book: *How can you lead your church without losing your soul?*

What do we mean by the phrase "losing your soul"? We do not mean that one loses his salvation or abandons her relationship with Christ. Our use of the phrase "losing your soul" refers to times of utter depletion of self when a church leader is set adrift by wave after wave of real and perceived pressures and no firm foothold seems to exist. According to Susan Muto and Adrian van Kaam, such stress-filled times leave us "ranging from physical exhaustion to spiritual aridity" while taking "more out of us than we have to give" (Muto and van Kaam, 2005, p. 9). Our observations reveal that church leaders in the depletion process tend to experience repeated episodes of explosive anger, treat all disagreements as personal attacks, and perceive any differences of opinion as personal challenges to their authority.

When we use the phrase "losing your soul" we also refer to periods of profound spiritual dryness that leave church leaders going through the motions of ministry while their hearts are far from it. Moreover we use this phrase to refer to times in leadership when something may happen right in the middle of tremendous fruitfulness in the local church that shatters momentum and distracts the focus of the entire organization. Such crises can have devastating effects on pastors, church leaders, and congregants alike. No matter what contributes to church leaders' loss of soul, at such times church leaders are in grave danger of acting in unholy ways. The purpose of this book is to show church leaders ways to develop spiritual, emotional, and relational stamina that will allow them to walk through the inevitable dark valleys of church crises *and* continue to grow in personal and social holiness.

# Relational Holiness Is Key

To borrow an idea from John Wesley, we believe that *relational holiness*[1] is central to preserving one's heart for ministry, even if it won't spare you from ministry's heartaches. For Mr. Wesley holiness was more than merely the salvation experience of the forgiveness of sin (Maddox, 1994). Holiness referred to "the presence or character of God reflected especially in the quality of [our] moral and spiritual lives" (Campbell and Burns, 2004, pp. 78-79). One might say that Wesley was keenly concerned about the quality of the lives we led while we were still on earth, in addition to the state of our immortal soul. Wesley pictured holiness as the here and now embodiment of God's love *within* the church and *to* the world. Holy living was not confined to the privacy of one's prayer closet. Instead, holy living was demonstrated in the ways in which believers related to others and served the world on a day-to-day basis.

Specifically, Wesley encouraged the people called Methodists to be holy in two complementary and inseparable ways: personally and socially. Personal holiness had to do with one's relationship with God. Social holiness had to do with how believers reflected God's love in their relationships with one another. Wesley could not imagine the one without the other. The love of God filled believers' hearts. Supported by this generous outpouring of love, believers' interactions with others were changed. Social holiness was not divorced from personal holiness. Quite the contrary, they stand in dynamic relationship with one another in such a way that personal and social holiness should be mutually reinforcing.

At this point, some readers may be tempted to put this book down because of past negative experiences with the idea of holiness. There indeed was a time when holiness was reduced to lists of dos and don'ts. Sadly, these efforts to fulfill the Great Commandment to love God and love neighbor in observable, measurable, and legalistic ways often led to what many experienced as unholy relationship dynamics. Rather than love forming holy relationships, rigid application of holiness standards became "deforming." Parenting became punitive (spare the rod and spoil the child); marriage became monitoring; church interactions became judgmental. Fear was the motivating emotion, not love. And as we know, "perfect fear casts out love." In this book we will suggest a different process for nurturing holiness. Instead of a rules-oriented process, we offer a growth-oriented process for developing *relational holiness*.

Putting this all together we propose that *church leaders with deepening levels of relational holiness are those whose identities are rooted and grounded in a vibrant and growing relationship with Christ. While such leaders also have vibrant and growing relationships with others, they are comfortable working closely with others in the church and they are capable of acting independently. These leaders model personal and social holiness in their everyday living as well as in the midst of difficult interpersonal relationships.* It is this kind of spiritual, emotional, and relational maturity, or relational holiness, that we believe makes a difference between losing heart and taking courage in stressful ministry settings. *v5.*

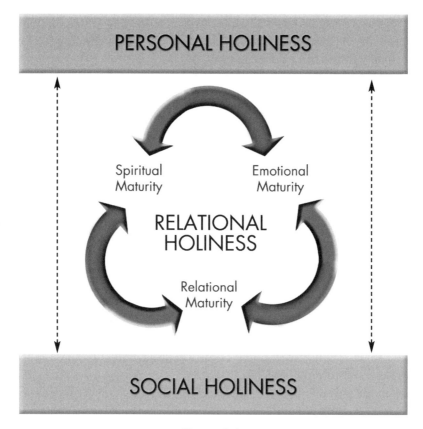

*Figure 1.1*

Please don't give up here! All of us must struggle with the issues surrounding our lack of holiness and lack of maturity, and certainly none of us will come to a point where further growth in the Lord is not needed. John Wesley recognized this in his call for his followers to go on to perfection. This text is about steps we are called to take that will enable the Lord to move us into the maturity and fruitfulness intended for all of us.

Relational holiness is revealed in three ways.[2] We see evidence of relational holiness in how we relate to God, in how we manage ourselves emotionally, and in how we relate to others, especially when those relationships become loaded with anxiety. As we grow in relational holiness, we become more mature in these three areas of life. Figure 1.1, above, pictures relational holiness. Unfortunately, when these three aspects of relational holiness are presented in a list, it can appear as if they are unrelated to one another. In reality they are intimately intertwined. Each aspect of relational holiness shapes the others. Spiritual, emotional, and interpersonal health are inseparable (Scazzero, 2003). Peter Scazzero, founding pastor of New Life Fellowship, New York City, declares that "*it is not possible for a Christian to be spiritually mature while remaining emotionally immature*" (p. 50).

# Relational Holiness: Spiritual Maturity

*First, church leaders with maturing levels of relational holiness are those whose identities are rooted and grounded in a vibrant and growing relationship with Christ.* The reality of an intimate and growing relationship with God can be heavily influenced for better or worse by the relationships we had with our parents when we were children. According to Adrian van Kaam and Susan Muto (2006), parents or parental substitutes have a key responsibility in instilling "the foundational triad of natural faith, hope, and love" (p. 61) in their children. When a parent expresses love toward their children by caressing them, smiling at them, paying attention to proper hygiene such as changing their diapers at appropriate times, and bathing them regularly, natural faith, hope, and love are instilled. These concrete expressions of love let children know that they are worthwhile, that there is confident hope for a good future for them, and that they are being held in a caring embrace of real love. This natural triad gives children a deep sense that life is good and that those ~~roots~~ responsible for them are both dependable and benevolent. These chil-~~l of~~ dren have imprinted upon their hearts "the certitude that someone is or ~~Faith~~ may be there for [them] at providential moments when [they] most need attention" (p. 61).

While attending graduate school in the mid-1980s, I (Steve) ran home for lunch one day to find a perfect example of the impartation of respectful faith, hope, and love. Upon entering the kitchen I found my wife on her hands and knees cleaning up a mess. Our fifteen-month-old son had pushed a chair up to the kitchen counter, crawled up onto the chair and grabbed a near-full pitcher of apple juice. Somehow, he got the pitcher (contents still intact) back down on floor level, took it over to the dog's food dish, and gave the dog an overflowing drink of apple juice. After cleaning the sticky floor, Diane looked down again and gasped. Oozing from the boy's pants and dripping onto the floor was a rather unpredictable and quite smelly substance. As I helped wipe the floor yet a second time I noticed the reactions of the mother by my side. She was comical about the boy giving the dog a drink. She didn't yell at her son. Yes, she was a little frustrated, but these were not unusual occurrences for her—in those days she spent a large part of her time cleaning up messes. I watched her lean down and then carefully pick up that messy, dripping little boy, place him in the sink, clean him off until he looked (and smelled) like new again, and finally pat his little shiny behind with a love, patience, and acceptance that were astounding to me.

In a few noontime moments, here was a mother imparting foundational faith, hope, and love into her child. Through her respectful presence, she was affirming him as a valued person of infinite worth, she was instilling a basic trust that he would grow and develop in goodness, and she was loving her adventurous son unconditionally. When parents, however, lack in their ability to consistently demonstrate natural faith, hope, and love in their children, their offspring may find it difficult "to believe that it is good to be alive nor hope that [they] will be able to enjoy a worthwhile future" (van Kaam and Muto, 2006, p. 61). In other words, the child may be left with a tragic inability "to trust in the end that all may be well" (p. 61).

In that every parent is either a son of Adam or a daughter of Eve, no parents have done their job perfectly of putting the spiritual root system of faith, hope, and love into their children. The theological doctrine of original sin broadcasts that none of us either escapes the deformation imparted through imperfect parenting nor escapes passing some level of deformation on to others. The good news of the gospel is that God both works through good parenting and despite poor parenting. In what John Wesley termed *prevenient grace* or the grace that always goes before us, we are drawn to the love of God. Then through *converting grace*, or the grace that turns our hearts in repentance toward God, we are placed in relationship with Jesus the Messiah. Christian baptism confirms these movements of grace in our lives and because it is a sacrament of our Lord; it offers a further avenue for grace to come into our hearts. In and through all of these movements of God's love, the Lord *infuses* what the church has historically called the theological virtues of faith, hope, and love into our graced, redeemed, and cherished lives.

The infused grace of *faith* enables us to not only affirm the lordship of Jesus but also to actually put the whole weight of our lives in ongoing actions of trusting surrender to him. Faith follows after and holds closely to a good savior. Infused *hope* gives us a supernatural assurance that

10

despite how things may appear at times, God really is good and can be trusted. *Hope* lives day by day with the assurance that in the end all shall be well[3] and in the everyday events of our lives, we shall see "the goodness of the LORD in the land of the living" (Ps 27:13). Hope affirms that God not only can but will bring goodness through the people, events, circumstances, and things of our lives. And God's infused love embraces us in such a transformational manner that we are able to both know him through the accepting, forgiving, and renewing love that he spills into our hearts and then enables us to return that very love not only back to him, but to those around us as well.

Faith, hope, and love continue to form the structure of our lives through the three-fold spiritual formation process of *purifying formation, illuminating reformation*, and *unifying transformation* (van Kaam and Muto, 2004), as will be discussed in detail in chapter 3. Suffice it to say for now that *purifying formation* comes when we allow the Holy Spirit to show us how a particular action or thought arose from our sinful nature. As the darkness in our own hearts is confronted, we are moved to sorrow over our transgression and ask the Lord for grace to leave such a fallen state of being behind. Through the gracious love of our Heavenly Father, we are then given a true desire to lead a Christlike life marked by faith, hope, and love.

*Illuminating reformation* begins unfolding a deeper way of life in Christ when we listen to and then are obedient to the directives we hear from the living word that is Jesus (John 1:14). As we humbly turn from ways that are not Christlike, our lives begin undergoing major restructuring. This wonderful reformation of heart and actions unfolds as we follow the light we have received from the Lord. We are careful on this path of discipleship to give proper attention to the means of grace that Wesley outlined for us, including prayer, searching the Scriptures, the Lord's supper, fasting, and Christian conferencing (Harper, 1995).

*Unifying transformation* is the amazing process where, through sheer grace, the very inner structures of our lives are transformed into something completely different than what they were. Whereas we tended to demonstrate more of a fragmented, disjointed, and fallen character (a divided heart), the varying aspects of our lives begin to come together in a unified whole that seeks to authentically live the love we have experienced through Christ. Not only are we gradually made whole in Christ, but also we are at the same time brought into an increasing union of likeness with the Trinity itself. This union of love automatically and naturally spills over into the relationships that we share with others in our families, in our church communities, and in the world.

These marvelous processes of relating to God show us deep in our hearts that the Lord actively wills goodness for each of us and that he is seeking to bring the full measure of the freedom that he wants us to know as his children. Our actual ongoing experiences of formation, reformation, and transformation let us know firsthand that we can be filled and motivated by a presence of love that actively seeks to embrace this mystery called the Trinity and at the same time share this goodness with others. And even if you may have had a near-complete deprivation of faith, hope, and love in your life as a child and you are having to slowly, ever so slowly and painfully, work through the restructuring of your life because of abuse and violence done against you, hear the good news. The Lord himself has faith in you (he believes in you); he knows of the amazing future that he went to untold lengths to acquire for you (he hopes in you). And his desire is to bring goodness into your life. God loves you and he wants to bring you into a union of likeness with himself that brings you the perfect freedom of a child at play under her mother's loving care! This God is good and is ever bringing faith, hope, and love into our lives through sanctifying grace to slowly unfold a transformed creation of beauty.

The path of moving *from* purifying formation *through* illuminating reformation so that we might come *to* a point of unifying transformation in Christ where faith, hope, and love radiate from our hearts and define our relationships will take us to a place of spiritual maturity and relational holiness. Just as a mature fruit tree fulfills its nature by producing its own kind of fruit in season, so will a spiritually mature person fulfill his or her purpose by producing amazing fruit that comes from knowing who he or she is in Christ. Such persons will be marked by their solidity in life in that their trust in God's goodness is unshakable. When they face difficult circumstances, their relationship with the Trinity is strong enough to overcome the fear, anxiety, and anger that tend to erupt from tense situations. They will exhibit dependence upon their Lord, knowing that they stand in continual need of the grace, strength, discernment, and love that only the Lord can provide. Such dependence allows them to then love and serve others with the joy-filled freedom of self-donating love. We affirm that this type of maturity can be known during this lifetime.

# Relational Holiness: Emotional Maturity

No matter what church leadership position we hold, we take our emotional self with us into this work. For some church leaders that is a blessing. These individuals like themselves for the most part and have confidence in themselves. They see leadership crises as challenges rather than obstacles because they have a sense that with God's help they will be able to handle the situation well enough. For others this is a burden. They find themselves overwhelmed by intense emotions when conflict arises. They fear that *this* is the time when God will abandon them. This hampers their ability to lead effectively because they are controlled by either excessive anxiety or extreme anger, or they may lack any emotional response at all, which others may perceive as uncaring.

In the 1950s and 1960s, pioneer family therapist Murray Bowen talked about these same emotional processes in a different way (Kerr and Bowen, 1988). Bowen defined emotional maturity as the ability to balance individuality and togetherness. Bowen proposed that "the individuality force propels an organism to follow its own directives, to be an independent and *distinct* entity. The togetherness force propels an organism to follow the directives of others, to be a dependent, connected, and *indistinct* entity" (Titelman, 2003, p. 20, emphasis added). Bowen's idea of togetherness is closer to the image of "stuck-togetherness" than it is to connectedness, community, or communion that are healthy ways of relating closely to others. How we experience our self, or our sense of self, is the result of how we negotiate the push and pull of the individuality and stuck-togetherness forces. Can we maintain a sense of self as a *distinct entity*, to borrow Bowen's terminology, or will the stuck-togetherness force overwhelm us so that we give up our uniqueness and become an *indistinct entity*?

In our attempt to manage the forces of individuality and togetherness, two other variables come into play, namely, anxiety and differentiation of self (Titelman, 2003). Bowen proposed that people experience anxiety when they are caught between the desire for individuality and the demands of stuck-togetherness. That is to say, anxiety arises when a person desires to think and act in a distinct way, but is being pressured to abandon that distinctiveness and follow the crowd (or the family or the committee) instead. Bowen made a distinction between acute anxiety and chronic anxiety. Acute anxiety is our fear response to a real threat. It is time limited and specific. Chronic anxiety is our fear response to an imagined threat. This fear of what might be is not time limited. Acute anxiety can be associated with specific relationship events, such as the impending death of a loved one, an upcoming pastoral recall vote, or a called meeting of the Staff Parish Relations Committee. Chronic anxiety can be associated with *any imagined* person-to-person interaction, such as the anxiety that surfaces if you imagine that someone will respond badly to what you have to say to them. Sometimes the anticipated scenarios do come true. Sometimes they do not. Our years of ministry have revealed that many ministry professionals live with acute and chronic anxiety ranging from low-grade anxiety, always just below the surface, to crippling, overwhelming anxiety. We believe that the negative impact of acute and chronic anxiety on church leaders is underestimated. Because we feel so strongly about this, we describe more fully in chapter 2 how anxiety can restrain relational holiness.

Differentiation of self is Bowen's remedy for the anxiety that can permeate our relationships. Biologically, differentiation is the process by which human cells multiply and divide, the process by which cells "differentiate" themselves from one another (i.e., become *distinct* cells rather than *indistinct* cells). Developmentally, *differentiation of self* is the emotional process by which a child moves from being symbiotically attached to the primary caregiver, usually the mother, to being an emotionally separate and *distinct* self in relation to others in the family unit. Relationally, differentiation of self is the ability to define your self within the context of intimate relationships without resorting to cutting others off to maintain your self or without being emotionally absorbed or fused with another in order to have any sense of self at all. You may link differentiation with the concept of interdependence in contrast to dependence or independence. Differentiation includes the ability to access your thinking to manage anxiety-driven emotions when you are experiencing internal turmoil.

At this point you may be wondering what all of this has to do with leadership. In our opinion it has everything to do with it! If spiritual maturity is the first element in keeping your soul alive during trying times in ministry, then emotional maturity is the second important element. How we conceptualize and manage our emotional lives will play a significant role in whether we soar with the eagles or not. We discuss differentiation of self in detail in chapter 4.

# Relational Holiness: Interpersonal Maturity

So far our portrait of relational holiness includes spiritual maturity and emotional maturity. A third element of relational holiness for ministry leaders includes interpersonal maturity, or how well we relate to others, especially during times of stress. In the church, relationships matter. Not surprisingly, we may experience optimal spiritual and emotional growth when we are in safe and secure relationships with others in the body of Christ (Shultz and Sandage, 2006). Relationships also matter because God designed our world in such a way that God's work happens in and through relationships. In church-speak we refer to this as our "ministry." Unfortunately we may underestimate the impact that acting in unholy ways toward others has upon our ministry.

One lens that will help us understand the ways our relationships tie us to one another will be that of family systems theory (Friedman, 1985; Richardson, 1996, 2005; Steinke, 1993, 1996). Many of the factors that affect family functioning also affect the functioning of the church family. While this may seem self-evident, the actual skill of thinking systemically is not necessarily intuitive to most of us. Most of us tend to think in individual-focused ways rather than systems-focused ways.

When challenged, leaders who operate out of an individual-focused frame of reference are more likely to respond defensively to angry challenges from others. They may blame and issue counteraccusations. They frequently feel misunderstood so that leadership issues easily develop into "us versus them" situations. What appears clear from an individual-focused perspective is how the *other* person is creating trouble and how that *other* person needs to change. In contrast, leaders who operate out of a systems-focused theory can and do experience anxiety and anger when they are challenged; however, they take responsibility for managing the intensity of their anxiety and anger, so that it doesn't control or drive their thinking. They are interested in the challenger's point of view, and are thinking about how *their own* actions may have contributed to creating this impasse. Then they are quick to admit their own contributions. They can express their understanding of the other's perspective without feeling like they are selling out. Leadership dilemmas are approached with a team mindset rather than the belief that "someone is out to get me."

From an individual-focused perspective, interest is paid to what happens within the mind and motivations of the *other* individual and why they chose the paths they did. If relationship problems arise, an individual-focused point of view seeks to find out who is at fault. The goal is to find someone to blame. Once blame has been assigned, then the obvious solution is to deal with that guilty individual in ways that will reduce the stress, strain, and pain that others feel. From this perspective "it is all about me" when things go well, and definitely "all about you" when they don't.[4]

A systems-focused perspective doesn't deny individual responsibility or culpability. People can, and do, act in ways for which they should be held accountable. Nor does this perspective lack interest in what another thinks and feels. A systems-focused frame places individuals squarely within the matrix of the relational pushes and pulls that surround them. The unit of interest is the web of connections within which individuals function. This web of connections includes who is involved on the contemporary scene *and* who has been involved historically. It seeks to know how the players influence or trigger one another within this relationship matrix. An individual is held accountable for his or her actions, but these actions are also seen as one segment in a long chain of an action-reaction-action cycle that may reach back through several generations. In a very real sense, thinking systemically embraces the idea that no person is an island. All are intertwined in mutually reciprocal cycles of giving and receiving—emotionally and behaviorally.

It is our premise that interpersonal maturity is one of the characteristics that makes a difference in whether church leaders lose their soul. The more interpersonally mature the church leader is, the greater will be her or his capacity to manage interpersonal conflicts and challenges without spilling blood. In fact, the church leader's maturity will encourage greater degrees of maturity within those congregants who operate under his or her leadership. We tackle a specific aspect of interpersonal maturity, triangulation, in chapter 5. Chapter 6 ties things together as we explore how relational holiness may shape healthy relationships.

# Wrapping Up

We hope that you are as excited about relational holiness as we are. A word of caution is in order. This will not be a book filled with the latest and greatest techniques for pastoral leaders to use to "fix" other people. While we do include things that you can do to foster spiritual, emotional, and interpersonal maturity, we do not see a recitation of techniques as our goal. Relational holiness is more a way of being in relationships than it is a way of doing relationships. A mature pastoral leader who is growing in relational holiness is likely to have success even if a specific technique is botched. An immature pastoral leader whose growth in relational holiness is stunted may implement a technique perfectly and be disappointed in the results. The how-to that we offer is how to allow the Holy Spirit to grow you up into the mature pastoral leader that God desires you to become. In our opinion, *that* will make all the difference in the world.

# CHAPTER TWO

# ANXIETY: THE GIFT THAT KEEPS ON GIVING

*Do not worry about tomorrow, for tomorrow will worry about itself.*
*Each day has enough trouble of its own. —Matthew 6:34 NIV*

I love my job—it's the people that drive me crazy." Amanda dismissed this thought as quickly as it came. She was the director of music ministries at Big Steeple Church, Anywhere, USA, and the Christmas season was right around the corner. This particular morning her mind was filled with items on her "to do" list: Had the church administrator written all the extra rehearsal times into the church's master calendar? What was happening with the publicity and ticket distribution for the public performances that drew thousands into the church during Advent? And costumes for the children's Christmas programs—was that mother who agreed to chair the costume committee doing anything about them yet? How many of these delegated details would she have to do this year because a volunteer dropped the ball? She remembered that a tiff was brewing between the members of the sanctuary orchestra and the praise band over an alleged comment made by an anonymous musician that had the leaders of both groups up in arms and insisting that Amanda "do something" about it, whatever "it" was. Amanda couldn't quite get her hands around that one. Too much finger pointing was going on. Why couldn't they act like adults?

As if these things weren't enough, she had to endure the weekly staff meeting today. Her stomach was in knots just thinking about it. The senior pastor must have some kind of inferiority complex, the way he liked to micromanage everything that involved worship. "Who knows what last minute changes he will 'suggest'?" thought Amanda. She recalled that last year she had revamped the sanctuary choir concert because of one of his "suggestions," which she heard as an order rather than an option. She wished that she could stand up for herself, but it just wasn't in her nature to do so. She loved music. She loved leading worship. She loved bringing others into the presence of the Lord through worship music of all kinds. But dealing with the people problems was something else altogether. She thought that her blood pressure must be through the roof because she sensed a slight tightening in her chest. She reached for the aspirin. She also felt another tension headache coming on.

Does any part of Amanda's situation strike a chord with you? We (Steve and Toddy) surely have our versions of it. What links our stories with Amanda's is not the size of the churches in which they took place, or the facts of the matter. A more common thread that runs deeply through our leadership dilemmas and Amanda's is *anxiety*. The *Merriam-Webster's Collegiate Dictionary* (2004) defines anxiety as "a painful or apprehensive uneasiness of mind usually over an impending or anticipated ill." Anxiety anticipates some type of trouble in the immediate or distant future. You may recall from chapter 1 that Murray Bowen identified another form of anxiety when he proposed that people feel anxious when they are caught between the demands of individuality and stucktogetherness. If you get below the facts of many troublesome situations, you are most likely to find that anxiety is either taking center stage or lurking in the wings.

Why should we pay attention to anxiety in a book about leadership? Quite simply because anxiety makes a huge difference in how church leaders frame problems. The higher the leader's anxiety the more likely it is that she will experience the problem as a crisis rather than as a challenge and opportunity for growth. In addition, anxiety affects how she leads. For example, when leaders get anxious, their ability to think clearly, calmly, and objectively is impaired. They are therefore more likely to make emotionally driven decisions at pivotal moments, the consequences of which may create more problems in the future than they solved in the anxious present. Their flexibility is hampered as their capacity to envision creative alternatives is reduced. Furthermore, highly anxious leaders tend to hunker down, batten down the hatches, or circle the wagons. Their ability to embrace differences of opinion is diminished while their demand for conformity is heightened. Moreover, they are more likely to respond to others with automatic knee-jerk reactions. Highly anxious leaders quickly shift into self-protective ways of relating to others. They become overly concerned with being liked and affirmed by others, which may lead some anxious leaders to worry excessively about what others think of them. Or they chafe against the standards and expectations that they believe others have for them, sometimes to the point of seeming rebellious.

Anxiety has an interesting set of connections with relational holiness. Anxiety can impede growth in all areas of relational holiness. Spiritually, anxiety tempts us to take our eyes off Jesus and focus instead on the storms of life that surround us. When we do this, the waves of anxiety swell and we are likely to sink below their surface. Emotionally, anxiety can dominate our emotional life to the point of becoming debilitating. Interpersonally, anxiety prompts us to react to others in ways that may actually harm the relationship. On the other hand, anxiety can be a source of valuable information. Spiritually, anxiety can point to areas of our lives that need the healing power of the Holy Spirit and an increase of faith, hope, and love. Emotionally, anxiety can alert us to *real* dangers. When this happens it means that we have paid appropriate attention to our anxiety and we have taken the right kind of remedial action. Interpersonally, anxiety can signal that tension exists within a group. This is an early warning signal that gives us a chance to decide how we want to respond. Anxiety can spur us on to deeper levels of personal or social holiness, or anxiety can stop us in our tracks and lead to sinful attitudes and actions.

The bottom line: anxious leaders look for ways to lessen their anxiety. While some anxiety-reduction strategies are healthy, other approaches end up making things worse. We believe that understanding and knowing how to manage one's anxiety is part of maturity, and that it is one of the things that will make a difference between saving one's soul and losing it in leadership. We wonder how many fine church leaders were driven out of their positions by persistent acute and chronic anxiety. In this chapter we will explore what anxiety looks like and how anxiety negatively affects church leaders and their congregations.

# What Does Anxiety Look Like?

What do you associate with anxiety? Perhaps you know about panic attacks, phobias, or post-traumatic stress disorder. These are the names of some psychological problems that are classified as anxiety disorders. To be eligible for these diagnoses, a patient must display particular symptoms for certain lengths of time under specific circumstances. People who experience these types of problems are often under the care of a physician, psychiatrist, psychologist, or other licensed mental health provider. Fortunately, we are *not* talking about this level of anxiety! The kind of anxiety we will be discussing in this chapter can indeed reach a point where one could be diagnosable, but more often than not, the type of anxiety that is our focus does not reach these critical levels. This does not make it is any less troublesome, however. If we aren't talking about clinical levels of anxiety, then what kind of anxiety are we talking about? Perhaps you could call it "relationship anxiety" to distinguish it from its clinical cousins. Following Murray Bowen (Kerr and Bowen, 1988), relationship anxiety occurs when we perceive our need for individuality is threatened by the demands of stuck-togetherness.[1]

How does this work? You may recall that individuality helps us define ourselves as separate from others—as a "distinct entity" in Bowen's words. We show our individuality through the beliefs, ideals, goals, and values that we embrace and embody. In contrast, stuck-togetherness moves us to abandon these values to attain the approval of others, to become an "indistinct entity." Stuck-togetherness compels us to conform to the expectations of others to become a part of the group. This could sound like Bowen was anticommunity. He wasn't. It was just that in his psychiatric practice he saw that more family problems developed when people merged with their family or cut off from their family (think of this as resistance to merging in the extreme). Departing a bit from classic Bowen theory, we suggest that *healthy togetherness*, what we would ideally think of in terms of community and connection at its best, makes room for individual differences without threatening to sever the emotional connection. *Unhealthy stuck-togetherness* makes no allowance for individual difference because difference is dangerous. Unhealthy stuck-togetherness demands conformity as the price for connection and approval.

Bowen theorized that families settle at a certain level of togetherness that is demanded from their members. For some families this is a healthy level of connectedness that in effect encourages individuality. For other families it is closer to an unhealthy level of stuck-togetherness. We grow up thinking that this balance of individuality and togetherness is normal. We become accustomed to it, and we seek that same level of togetherness in our adult relationships. That is to say that like Goldilocks we seek to find that "just right" balance of togetherness and individuality in our relationships. We make adjustments when the relationship gets "too hot" or "too cold" for our liking. When the balance gets out of whack, we experience relationship anxiety. We want more individuality while others are demanding that we conform. Or we want others to conform and they resist our attempts to draw them closer. Church leaders are notorious for the latter in that we do have a high calling from our Lord and a burning vision for the good of those we serve. This readily becomes sick, however, when we insist upon conformity.

Bowen first observed these dynamics in families. But soon his observations were applied to other arenas. When people interact on a regular basis, as many church staff members do, they inevitably create a "dance" where each one moves in ways to maximize his or her comfort zone of individuality and togetherness. If one person's maximum is another person's minimum, then someone steps on his partner's toes in the midst of this relationship tango. This would be the case with Amanda and her senior pastor. Amanda experiences the senior pastor as wanting more togetherness than she wants. He wants to have input into "her area." She experiences this as micromanaging. Her anxiety is evident in her failure to stand up for herself (she loses part of her individuality to keep peace with her pastor), her headache, and her dread of the weekly staff meetings. She is overly focused on what the pastor wants, and because she believes that she has no other option, she resentfully and anxiously gives in to his ideas. Of course, since it takes two to tango, we could also explore this from the senior pastor's perspective. He may experience Amanda as talented but insecure, with untapped leadership potential. He longs to delegate responsibility to her without his supervision, but her anxious self-presentation comes across to him as a cry for help. So he rides to her rescue and makes suggestions. That she always implements them is proof that she wants him to continue in this pattern.

Relationship anxiety directs our actions more often than we are aware of. For instance, imagine that someone who is important to you gets intensely angry with you and emotionally pulls away from you if you won't agree with him. His pulling away threatens the degree of closeness that you desire to have with him. Yet if you give in to his demand to change, then the degree of individuality that you desire is threatened. You are caught between a rock and a hard place. Is maintaining your link with this important person worth the price of losing some measure of individuality? Or to say it another way, is sticking to your position worth the price of losing this valuable relationship? This is a highly common scenario in ministry. While you may very much want and need the support of an influential person within your congregation, you may find yourself staggering when that person fails to support an important ministry initiative of yours.

We need individuality and connection to be fully functioning human beings. This is how God created us. From infancy throughout adulthood, we seek an optimal, personalized balance between individuality and togetherness in our relationships. For some of us the accent is on individuality. For others it is on togetherness. When our relationships are running smoothly and the tension is low, it is relatively easy to keep our different needs for individuality and togetherness in balance. However, if I want connection and you move too far away or I want space and you move too close, then I am kicked out of my comfort zone and I experience relationship anxiety in my scramble to regain my preferred balance. We experience these negotiations most powerfully in our relationships with our family. We also bring our preferences for individuality and togetherness into other contexts, such as in the church, although perhaps in less intense ways. Less intense, that is, until crisis or conflict erupt.

Regarding relationship anxiety, Ronald Richardson (1996) observes that

> at its most basic level, anxiety is about threat to the loss of who we are—our 'self'. . . . As adults . . . we can feel as though our survival depends on others. . . . At a deep level, we think we will perish unless the important people in our lives provide what we think we need from them emotionally [closeness or distance]. If they don't, we feel threatened. Our sense of self is incomplete, or under attack. (pp. 48-49)

Most of the time, we are not aware that these processes are in play. However, when they are triggered, we react. When anxiety is high, the repertoire of automatic responses may include blaming, accusing, demanding my rights, and focusing on who is in because they agree and who should be out because they disagree. It can also include other automatic responses like feeling tongue-tied, feeling like your brain is turning off just when you need it most, or emotionally tuning out. You might take a moment to think about how you tend to respond when someone wants more of you than you are willing to give (for example, the senior pastor says to Amanda, "Tell me the details of your plans for music during Advent." Amanda says to the senior pastor, "I haven't quite worked everything out yet. You know how spontaneous I can be during worship").

You may have noticed that we have not mentioned the anxiety that arises when you try to meet competing demands, such as the anxiety that comes when church leaders try to balance the time they should devote to their families and the time they are devoting to their leadership responsibilities. This kind of anxiety is different from what the focus of this book is. If this type of anxiety rules your world, we suggest that you pick up a copy of Anthony J. Headley's *Achieving Balance in Ministry*. You will find many wonderful suggestions within its pages to help you bring balance to your life. On the other hand, we also believe that church leaders will be in a better position to act on Dr. Headley's recommendations when they are also able to manage their relationship anxiety. For us then the question becomes this: how often does a church leader say yes to a new task because of a need to please or not disappoint another person by saying no? This is more indicative of a problem with relationship anxiety than time management.

# The Anatomy of Anxiety

From our discussion so far it can appear as if relationship anxiety is like this thing that comes out of nowhere and controls you and your relationships. Or perhaps our discussions have painted its portrait as so shapeless, formless, and vague that you can't wrap your mind, let alone your hands, around it. For others our discussion of anxiety may have the appearance of psychobabble. It may be helpful to understand the neurological basis of anxiety. In this section we explore how anxious brains develop. In a later section we expand these insights to see how anxious brains operate within the contexts of close relationships. As you read this section, keep in mind that Murray Bowen developed his theory of human relationships in the 1950s and 1960s. The technology to study the brain in the way that we can today did not exist for Bowen. He could not have known how truly ahead of his time he was when he developed his theory about the role that anxiety played in human relationships.

Your brain is organized into three major systems. The oldest system in your brain includes your brain stem and its related parts. It is often referred to as the "reptilian brain" or the "old brain." This system operates on the basis of instinctive reactions. It controls your breathing, heart rate, blood pressure, and so on. We normally view these processes as being outside of our conscious control. In other words, you normally don't tell your heart to beat or your lungs to expand and contract. They do so automatically under the guidance of the old brain. The second system of your brain is the emotional brain. It includes those parts that regulate emotions and the memories or experiences that are associated with emotionally laden events. The emotional brain comes "online" at birth, although it is not fully developed. The emotional brain's sensitivity to life in general and to social interactions in particular is shaped by experiences within the family during infancy. In other words, parenting impacts the physical development of a baby's brain. This part of your brain evaluates the degree to which you are safe or in danger; whether life is painful or pleasurable; whether this or that is something you want to embrace or something you want to avoid. Finally, there is the thinking brain system, also called the neocortex. This part of your brain operates on the basis of conscious thought. You make decisions, consider alternatives, and chart courses of action with the thinking brain.

These three brain systems share information, sending and receiving neural impulses from lower sections of the brain to higher sections, that is, from the old brain up to the thinking brain, and vice versa, from the thinking brain back down to the old brain. Raw data for decisions is sent up to the thinking brain, that is, instinctive reactions and emotional responses become what the thinking brain uses to make decisions. Then based on the decisions made by the thinking brain, directions are sent back down to the emotional brain and the old brain.

The systems of your brain work at different speeds and by different mechanisms. The old brain and the emotional brain take what might be called the "low road," while the thinking brain takes the "high road" (Goleman, 2006). You are born with low-road processing. The low road activates relatively simple responses (fight or flight) at rapid-fire speeds (Cozolino, 2006). The systems of your brain that travel the low road are easily excited. They do not wait for a full analysis of a situation before jumping to conclusions. They need only the *gist* of a situation. Low-road parts of your brain operate on the basis of fixed responses. Their typical pattern is "fire, ready, aim." Their job is to *initiate action*. For example, you are walking in the woods and see an object across your path. Before you have time to think, your emotional brain has activated all of the "SNAKE alarm systems."

Conversely, the high road of the thinking brain is built to manage complex situations. Its responses are learned over time and it *slowly* processes data it receives from sense organs, liberally augmented by information from the emotional brain. The thinking brain looks for details that differentiate one thing from another so that it can make the best possible *choice* of action. Its pattern is "ready, aim, fire." Going back to your stroll through the woods, your low-road emotional brain has launched the flight reaction in response to the sensory data about that thing on the path before your high-road thinking brain has had a chance to evaluate the situation. You jump back or stop in your tracks. At that point your thinking brain takes the reins back, reviews all incoming data, and concludes, "It's only a tree limb!" You continue your walk.

You can see that the emotional brain and the thinking brain are two systems that are designed by God to work in tandem to help us negotiate life's circumstances. But herein lies a problem. Because the emotional brain operates on the rapid-fire low road, it is capable of "emotional hijacking" (Goleman, 1995). The emotional brain works off the essence or general idea of a situation. It instantaneously draws upon its storehouse of emotional memories for those that are a good enough fit with the present situation. God has created us so that negative emotional information is stored widely across your brain, is anchored more firmly into your brain, and is recalled more rapidly than positive emotional information. As a result, our brain can trigger anxiety, and its related physiological manifestations, in the twinkling of an eye so that by the time the thinking brain comes online, a whole series of body reactions have been launched by the emotional brain. Unless the thinking brain is primed to take control and slow things down, it will react to the emotional brain's data with the conclusion, "I am in danger!" And *that* is all that the emotional brain needs to continue revving up.

But how does this relate to church leadership? An example will help this become clearer. Imagine that Amanda comes from a family in which her every breath seemed to be monitored by her parents (high demand for stuck-togetherness). She enters adulthood sensitive to authority figures who metaphorically breathe down her neck. She longs for more space (desire for individuality), but she doesn't know how to stand up for herself (individuality). When she thinks about asserting herself, she is overwhelmed by the fear of losing the approval (stuck-togetherness) of other people. She carries this fear with her into ministry. Her experience with her senior pastor mirrors her experience with her parents closely enough that her emotional brain launches into anxious action as soon as thoughts of "staff meeting" come up. These warning signals include physiological sensations such as dry mouth, sweaty palms, and a more rapidly beating heart. Using the low road, these signals are sent on to the thinking brain.

Unfortunately, Amanda's emotional reactions have gotten to the metaphorical finish line long before her thinking brain had a chance to think things through. So she concludes, "Oh, no, another dreaded staff meeting. What will go wrong this time?" Based on this cognitive assessment, the emotional brain continues to send out fear messages and the old brain continues to sustain the body's fight-or-flight response. The thinking brain subsequently decides that this is going to be a horrible meeting. The only thing that Amanda is aware of is her sense of impending doom and her dread of going to the staff meeting. Between now and when she is in the staff meeting, the three parts of her brain will engage in this exquisite dance of sending data and receiving directions. Based on her current level of awareness, Amanda will enter the staff meeting filled with relationship anxiety and vulnerable to continued emotional hijacking by her emotional brain.

# When Relationships Get Messy: Anxiety and Emotional Gridlock

Let's visit Amanda's staff meeting. Amanda, the senior pastor, and the rest of the leadership team sit in the senior pastor's office. The task at hand is to review plans for the Advent and Christmas season. Given all that happens at Big Steeple Church during the Advent season, it is essential that each member of the leadership team keep the big picture in mind as they work out their individual responsibilities. The senior pastor leads the discussion. Each staff member discusses Advent plans and programs as they relate to the various areas of the church. Amanda feels her tension level rise as her turn to share comes closer. Her mouth is dry. Her palms are sweaty. She takes a moment to review her outline, and is further dismayed when she cannot find the paper that contains her detailed notes. As she shuffles through the stack of papers in her lap, she suddenly realizes that it is her turn to speak. She stumbles through the schedule of choir rehearsals and performances, annoyed that she sounds so tentative. Of course, the senior pastor had his suggestions to make. She resigns herself to the inevitable. Amanda changes things to avoid any disagreement. She finds that this is less troubling to her than challenging him. That would take too much out of her.

Family therapist David Schnarch (1997, 2002) has identified two anxiety-related relationship patterns that he refers to as "gridlock" and the "two-choice dilemma." While his application is to intimate relationships, such as marriage, we propose that similar dynamics are at work in other ongoing relationships, such as those among church leadership teams. Schnarch observes that people in enduring relationships regularly reach points of tension and disagreement. On the surface this tension appears to relate to decisions that the people in these relationships must reach, or the content of their disagreement. Underneath the surface the tension relates to the anxiety people feel when someone is demanding more conformity than the other wants to grant.

Many times people will use the strategy of "agree to disagree" to resolve the impasse and restore balance. Schnarch (1997, 2002) observes that this maneuver doesn't work when action or behavior of some kind is involved. In such cases, you have a "winner" (the person who gets his or her way) and a "loser" (the person who wanted to do something else). As long as the "loser" does not care deeply about the issue, no problem exists. For example, from Amanda's perspective she either abides by her senior pastor's wishes or she doesn't. If Amanda has no emotional investment in the music selection, then abiding by the senior pastor's musical preferences causes her no anxiety. But that is not the case here. Amanda cares deeply about the musical selection (individuality) for Advent and she experiences anxiety when the senior pastor makes changes in her program (stuck-togetherness).

These types of situations can eventually lead to *gridlock* (Schnarch 1997, 2002). When people are gridlocked, they feel dismissed and misunderstood. A hope, dream, ideal, or expectation is at stake. The delicate balance between the desire for individuality and demand for togetherness has been threatened. When you hit gridlock in your relationships, you begin to function on automatic pilot in such a way that you merely *react* to the other person, just as they are *reacting* to you.

Schnarch (1997, 2002) further proposes that people then find themselves facing the *two-choice dilemma*. He observes that when people are gridlocked they are anxious about not getting what they want *and they are anxious about how the other person may react if they go about getting what they want*. It is at this point that people want to exercise two choices as a way to lower their anxiety. They want the choice to follow their own desired course of action (choice 1) and they want to control how the other will react to their choice (choice 2). In Amanda's case she wants to maintain her musical selections *and* she wants a guarantee that the senior pastor will approve of her musical selections from the beginning *or* she wants a guarantee that the senior pastor will *readily and happily* back down if she stands up to him. What she fears is that the senior pastor would respond with disdain, disapproval, and distance if she were to defend her selections.

The problem is that we do *not* have the option to control how others will react to us. We do *not* want to accept that we have only one choice—to act or to not act—and then to deal with the other person's response, whatever that may be.

When we want to avoid acting and dealing with the other's response, Schnarch (1997, 2002) proposes that three options now lie before us. One option is to dominate, or take over, the other person through various forms of intimidation or control. Some of us can take over with logic. We use our words to back others into a corner and leave them with no room to move other than the way we want them to go. "Takeover" can also assume the form of emotional intensity so that others are overwhelmed by us. Taking over doesn't have to be a hostile takeover. It can also come across as overbearing caring, a "bless your heart, here, let me do that for you and don't bother yourself about it" kind of takeover.

A second option is to give ourselves over to the other's desire. This is Amanda's pattern in the staff meeting. She just caves in to the wishes of the senior pastor. Giving over can give the appearance of compromise and negotiation. In contrast, with true compromise both parties relinquish some aspect of what they want, but they do not feel diminished or wounded as a person in the process. When we give over we are *giving up something of our self as an anxious response to appease the other and maintain the status quo*. That is, we are willing to sacrifice an important aspect of our individuality in the face of the other's demand for stuck-togetherness.

Perhaps you know these first two patterns by other names. Murray Bowen (Kerr and Bowen, 1988) called them patterns of "over functioning" and "under functioning." Recovery communities would link "taking over" with the term "enabling." More recently, these patterns have been called patterns of "over responsibility" and "under responsibility" (Gilbert, 1992; Richardson, 1996). Whatever you call them, please be aware that church leaders are especially susceptible to these patterns. While one of the tasks of the church leader is to equip the saints for the work of the ministry (Eph 4:12-13), many church leaders find it hard to bear when the saints let them down. Over-functioning church leaders believe in delegating responsibilities, but they worry, fuss, and hover when they do so. For example, Amanda delegated the responsibility for the children's costumes but fretted about her lack of control over the matter.

Is it hard (i.e., anxiety provoking) for church leaders to let important tasks go and risk them not being done right or not being done at all? Of course, it is! But the flip side is that over-responsible church leaders tend to pair up with under-responsible parishioners.[2] We might be tempted to ask, *Which came first—the under-responsible parishioner or the over-responsible leader?* The systemic answer would be, *It doesn't matter which came first. What matters is that now they are reinforcing each other.*

Schnarch's (1997, 2002) third option is to withdraw emotionally or physically from the relationship. Bowen called this "cutoff" (Gilbert, 1992; Kerr and Bowen, 1988; Titelman, 2003). From a Bowenian perspective, cutoff is a reactive response to unwanted bids for stuck-togetherness. What does cutoff look like? We emotionally shut down and shut the other out. We get up and leave the room. We stop listening. We do not participate. And an infinite number of variations to those three strategies exist. As different as they appear, they have one thing in common. They represent knee-jerk responses to the relationship anxiety generated by demands for stuck-togetherness.

When people employ any of these three strategies to manage relationship anxiety, we find that their relationship suffers. People exercise these options when they feel unsafe. When people feel unsafe, they feel more anxious. When they feel more anxious, they begin to look to others to change to make their anxiety go away. They conclude, "I'm anxious. You change. You need to do something to make me feel better." It is when we shift the burden of responsibility for our emotional composure onto their shoulders that problems arise. This is where Amanda is in her relationship with her senior pastor. She doesn't want to do something different. She wants him to change so that she will be comfortable. Anxiety often demands conformity and punishes difference. An urge to find a scapegoat emerges rather than taking a look at how one and all have contributed to the stress that currently permeates the relationship. In chapters 4 and 5 we will look at healthier ways to deal with the anxiety that fuels the two-choice dilemma.

What happens when anxiety floods a system? Family therapist Walter Howard Smith (2003) observes that as stress and anxiety increase, we are more likely to organize our lives around our anxiety-avoiding strategies. As stress and anxiety rise, people will alter their beliefs, change the degree to which they are close to or distant from one another, and change their behavior. The greater and more persistent the levels of anxiety, the more they will direct their actions toward reducing anxiety, stress, and conflict. This will often take the form of pressure for conformity and a minimization of difference to achieve or maintain unity. In the face of anxiety, different is *not* good. Of course, the pressure to conform can elicit resistance from those who are expected to cave in. When anxiety floods a system, people are not able to think clearly about their options. Nor can they develop reasonable plans of action. When key church leaders feel threatened and unsafe, this reverberates through the congregation. Anxiety tends to "heighten emotional [exchanges], so that people who feel threatened and anxious are especially prone to catching other people's emotions" (Goleman, 2006, p. 39).

# Relationship Anxiety—The Gift That Keeps on Giving

Let's go back to Amanda for a moment. Can you see the anxiety in her relationships? Amanda reacted anxiously when she thought about her senior pastor (gave over), when she imaged the tiff between the music directors (perhaps withdrawal), and when she wondered what was happening with the children's costumes (desire to take over). While it is possible for Amanda to be the only anxious person on her church staff, we find this highly unlikely. The others with whom she works will pick up her unease (Cozolino, 2006; Goleman, 2006). As we will discuss in this section, relationship anxiety is the gift that keeps on giving.

God created humanity in such a way that when one person is anxious, others sense it and their anxiety alarms will also be tripped. This is why we think of anxiety as the gift that keeps on giving! Let me (Toddy) give you an example of how infectious anxiety is. A friend and I were working a double shift in our church's nursery one Sunday. This meant that we would be with our charges for approximately 2½ hours. This particular Sunday we had a full house—seven little ones between the ages of twelve and twenty-four months. All of these children were regulars in the nursery. My friend and I were not strangers to them. Shortly after everyone had arrived and all were quietly playing, one of the children started to cry. "Cry" doesn't quite capture it. This particular child didn't cry; this child screamed. Soon we had a chain reaction of tears. In dismay, my friend and I watched each baby listen, look around, and start to cry. It wasn't too long before we had seven crying toddlers. Periodically everyone calmed down. But it only took one sniffle to begin the process again. This cycle happened about every fifteen minutes. Eventually we threw in the towel and called several mothers back to the nursery.

What happened? Scientists who study the brain have identified parts of our brain that are called mirror neurons (Goleman, 2006). These neurons reflect the emotions of others. For the babies in our nursery that morning, their mirror neurons were working overtime. If one baby was anxious, the mirror neurons of the other six registered anxiety. Each of our formerly content but now anxious charges looked around the nursery to find the face of their mother or father. Unfortunately, they only saw the faces of the two nursery workers. We were not who they wanted! The moral of this story: anxiety is as contagious as the flu, and it only takes a whiff to get the ball rolling. This process is true for adults as well as children, and it happens in staff meetings and among the members of administrative boards as well as in the nursery. Family therapist Edwin Friedman (1985) likens this emotional reactivity to a serial electrical system. In a serial system, all lights operate off a single line. If there is disruption anywhere in the electrical system, it is felt everywhere in the system. Perhaps you are the proud owner of an ancient set of Christmas lights, which function as a serial electrical system. Either all lights are on, or all lights are off. As a child I spent many hours of trial and error in an attempt to find that one burned-out lightbulb on the string. That's what happened in the nursery. And this is what happens at many of our churches.

# How Do You Spell "Relief"?

Anxiety is unavoidable. It is as much a part of life as breathing. The problem is that few of us know how to manage our relationship anxiety in ways that nurture maturity. Sadly, the common strategies that we reviewed in this chapter are guaranteed to neither neutralize anxiety nor help church leaders grow spiritually, emotionally, or relationally. These tactics are only guaranteed to keep leaders anxious.

In spite of all the bad press that we gave anxiety in this chapter, anxiety does serve a useful purpose. It alerts us to things to which we need to pay attention. It can signal places where change needs to happen inside of us through purifying formation and illuminating reformation and in our relationships with others. Rather than view anxiety as a harbinger of doom, perhaps we can offer a different metaphor, one that points to the change potential that is latent in anxiety, even an invitation to spiritual transformation. Consider that leadership is like a crucible. A crucible can be thought of as a severe test, or series of tests, through which someone comes. If the person is overcome by the testing, then much is lost for the leader and for the organization. That has been the message of chapter 2. However, if the test is negotiated successfully, the leader emerges the stronger for it and the entire organization is blessed.

A crucible is also a container for transformation. From this perspective, a crucible is a vessel made of heat-resistant material that is used for chemical reactions that require high temperatures. How does this work? Two substances, such as two different metals, are placed in the crucible. The crucible is subjected to intense heat. The heat unleashes a chemical reaction within the crucible. If the generated force is stronger than the container, then the crucible cracks, and the transformation process is arrested. However, if the crucible is stronger than the force that is generated within it, then the original materials are transformed. We propose that leadership is a crucible into which leaders and their followers are thrust. When things heat up, as they inevitably will, leaders and those they lead experience anxiety. But notice that this anxiety contains within it the *potential for spiritual, emotional, and interpersonal transformation*, for going on to maturity in Christ. The question that is before us is this: What processes will ensure that the leadership crucible is strong?

That is the focus of the next few chapters! Our ultimate goal is to be able to experience the anxiety that comes with leading and to allow it to transform us. In this way we will be able to experience the kind of strength that we see in Paul:

> We are hard pressed on every side, but not crushed; perplexed, but not in despair; persecuted, but not abandoned; struck down, but not destroyed. . . . Rather, as servants of God we commend ourselves in every way: in great endurance; in troubles, hardships, and distresses; in beatings, imprisonments and riots; in hard work, sleepless nights and hunger; in purity, understanding, patience, and kindness; in the Holy Spirit and in sincere love; in truthful speech and in the power of God;

with weapons of righteousness in the right hand and in the left; through glory and dishonor, bad report and good report; genuine, yet regarded as impostors; known, yet regarded as unknown; dying, and yet we live on; beaten, and yet not killed; sorrowful, yet always rejoicing; poor, yet making many rich; having nothing, and yet possessing everything. (2 Corinthians 4:8-9; 6:4-10 NIV)

CHAPTER THREE

# RELATIONAL HOLINESS: SPIRITUAL MATURITY

*And we all, who with unveiled faces contemplate the Lord's glory, are being transformed into his image with ever-increasing glory, which comes from the Lord, who is the Spirit.—2 Corinthians 3:18 TNIV*

Not long ago, I (Steve) found myself standing on top of Mount Nebo in Jordan. I was leading a group of seminary students and friends of our institution on a tour of the Holy Lands when we arrived atop the mountain where Moses saw the promised land but was prevented from entering therein (see Deut 34:1-8). I knew ahead of time this would be an emotional place for me. For one thing, my heart hurt for Moses and the disappointment he must have felt at being prohibited by the Lord from entering the very goal of his life's mission and journey. He had toiled for some forty years to be able to enter into the land and could see it there stretching out before him across the Jordan River. He died on the mountain with the vision of a beautiful homeland before him and the steady hope in his heart that the Israelites would indeed enter into a land given to them by the Lord their God.

As I stood looking across the northern end of the Dead Sea, the Jordan Valley, the hills of the Judean wilderness, and the region around Bet Shean, Israel, I was filled with awe over the historical impact of the mountain and the pressing issue of finishing well in life and ministry. While gazing out over the Jordan Valley toward Jerusalem, I sensed the Holy Spirit pressing me with the transformational issue of spiritual maturity and I experienced a renewed longing to fulfill the purposes of God for my life. Within that longing I hungered to know the Lord face-to-face just as Moses had. I wanted, as well, to be able to share the richness of God's presence with the primary loved ones of my life and all of those I am called to serve as a church leader. I yearned to live in the reality of relational holiness.

Relational holiness issues a clarion call to followers of Jesus in general and church leaders in particular to attend purposefully to their relationship with the Triune God. We who have spent many years serving God in leadership positions know how easy it is to "play church," to fake inward transformation with outward manifestations of spiritual maturity. We become so busy doing things for God that we fail to guard time to be with God. The result is that soon church leaders have fastened their identity to the things of this world (status, power, prestige, and so on) and thereby become more susceptible to being cast adrift in the seas of anxiety. The alternative is to secure one's identity in Christ so that we become more like Jesus with each passing day. This is the heart of spiritual maturity. Relational holiness beckons church leaders to enter the promised land of likeness to the Lord.

The depth of relationship that Moses had with the Lord was of such an impacting nature that it literally transformed his appearance. Exodus 34:29 reports, "Moses did not know that the skin of his face shone because he had been talking with God." He had what van Kaam and Muto (2005) describe as an "epiphanic radiance" (p. 132). *Epiphanic* comes from the word *epiphany*, meaning "unveiling" or "showing." For example, one epiphany of Jesus was his presentation in the temple as recorded in Luke 2:22-28. This event was the revealing to the world of the mystery of God's love incarnate in a baby boy. It was a showing of divine goodness to all of those like Simeon and Anna who had the eyes of faith to behold the light of the world. Liturgically, the holiday of Epiphany is celebrated on January 6, which commemorates the coming of the Magi to adore the Christ child.

The epiphanic radiance that had shone forth from Moses' face resulted from his entering into "the fullness of God's light" (van Kaam and Muto,

2005, p. 132). Just as Moses reflected the radiant glory of the Lord into the lives of those he led, we, too, are called to allow the light of the Trinity to so permeate our hearts that the radiance of God shines outwardly into the lives of those we are called to serve. The royal path of relational holiness begins with deep immersion into the love of God before it can ever truly extend outward to the community around us. This is the foundation of spiritual maturity.

I (Steve) experienced this awareness anew as I stood on Mount Nebo. I was called once again to allow the fair light of Christ's love to be my light, my life, and my love. I was beckoned to share in his epiphany and to find the meaning and the fulfillment of my existence in him. There was a renewed call to union with the Trinity.

# Finding Our Identity in Christ

To be one with God and to find and to know our identity in and through Christ is the greatest invitation any of us can ever receive. No one can serve God as a church leader without risk of spiritual, emotional, and interpersonal exhaustion if one's identity is not found in and through Christ. This call to union is nothing short of a sharing in the uncreated light or glory that is the Godhead. Jesus' prayer in John 17:22-23 highlights this divine invitation:

> The glory that you have given me I have given [those who believe in Christ through the apostolic preaching and teaching], so that they may be one, as we are one, I in them and you in me, that they may become completely one, so that the world may know that you have sent me and have loved them even as you have loved me.

This invitation to be in Christ even as Jesus himself is in his Heavenly Father is the only true pathway to being truly human. All who love the Son of God are caught up within the eternal embrace of Father, Son, and Holy Spirit.

Church leaders face the daily temptation to present a façade to those they serve, to exhibit a "glittering image" of spiritual maturity (Howatch, 1987). Fear fuels the false images that we construct for one another. However, when we are embraced by the love of God, fear flees. In 1 John 4:16-18 we read these familiar words:

God is love. Whoever lives in love lives in God, and God in him [or her]. In this way, love is made complete among us so that we will have confidence on the day of judgment, because in this world we are like [Jesus]. There is no fear in love. But perfect love drives out fear, because fear has to do with punishment. (NIV)

Obviously, those we lead are not able to love us with the perfect love of God. Nonetheless, when we enter the promised land of likeness to the Lord, there is no need to fear either annihilation (the total loss of self-identity) or a stifling of personhood (the suppression of true freedom and joy). Rather, there is every reason to expect an ongoing unfolding of the deepest fulfillment imaginable. This sense of well-being only comes from being loved for who we are and cleansed of the brokenness and sinfulness that causes us to hunger and thirst for God. And as we live into this sense of well-being, we experience a surprising joy and an immense sense of fulfillment that comes from being instruments in bringing wholeness to others. This is our call as church leaders.

Union with the Trinity results in our inner contradictions being transformed into a very real purity of thought and deed in much the same way as when an orchestra is brought together through tuning to a single note and through playing a harmonious score together. Union with the Trinity also results in an outpouring of love toward those in our circle of kinship and friendship, and to whatever extent is possible, to a fallen world. Harmony of relationships grow as communion in Christ deepens. All of this involves the flowering freedom of personhood known as spiritual maturity.

Theologian Stephen Seamands (2005) writes:

> Someday what Jesus prayed for and what we already know now in part will be known in full. At the consummation there will be, as John Wesley describes it, "a deep, an intimate, an uninterrupted union with God; a constant communion with the Father and his Son Jesus Christ, through the Spirit; a continual enjoyment of the Three-One God. . . ." As the apostle Peter says, "participants of the divine nature" (2 Peter 1:4). Of course, this participation doesn't mean that our personal identity is lost in God or that our human nature actually becomes divine. God dwells in us and we dwell in God, but our radical divine-human differences are never blurred, nor do we ever merge with one another. Yet what a rich, joyous union with the triune God is offered to us. (p. 12)

Thus with neither annihilation nor suppression of self but with restoration of personhood and the strength that comes through a unity of love with the very wellspring of love itself, my true self—what the early church called the *imago Dei* (the image of God), which is our soul, our deepest identity, begins to spread its wings and to know its own nature through its union with the One who created and redeemed it. The infused theological virtues of faith, hope, and love (gifts from the Lord that permeate our being) become our nature along with all of the gifts graciously bestowed by the Holy Spirit and the varying graces given by God (such as forgiveness, enlightenment, and calling, as well as family, friends, and the whole of creation itself). And all of these things are clearly seen in Jesus whom we name as the Savior. Moreover, all of these realities flow from him into any and all who love his name and who submit their hearts to his love. Who I am as a creature (one created by someone other than myself) becomes completely embedded in and defined by who Jesus was and is and will continue to be. My identity is found in his nature even as he shares that nature with me through an ongoing transformational process that results in relational holiness.

On top of Mount Nebo, I (Steve) longed to live in the land of likeness with God's love and I yearned for the wholeness that can only come through oneness of heart with the Lord's heart and will. I wanted to know myself through his characteristics, not through the corruption of my personal sinfulness. As such, Mount Nebo brought a sense of finitude to mind as it pressed the twin issues of brokenness and sinfulness to mind. I recalled how the people of Israel simply could not endure "the glory of [Moses'] face" (2 Cor 3:7) after he came down from Mount Sinai with the Ten Commandments. But I also remembered how that glorious presence came to an end (2 Cor 3:13). The long journey in the desert wilderness, the continual conflict with enemies without and disruptions within, and the strain of leadership in unstable times all wore on Moses' soul and no doubt created anxiety within his life. And then one day, the heaviness of his situation gave him the excuse to disobey the Lord. In a fit of anger Moses struck the rock at Meribah rather than commanding it "to yield its water" as the Lord had instructed him (Num 20:8). The Lord then rebuked both Aaron and Moses, saying, "Because you did not trust in me, to show my holiness before the eyes of the Israelites, therefore you shall not bring this assembly into the land that I have given them" (Num 20:12).

If it could happen to Moses, it can also happen to today's church leaders. Most of us in Christian ministry have known the searing trials and desert waste places of a long journey home. While Christian ministry is never devoid of the joy of our risen Lord, there are also times when the cross of suffering bears heavily upon us. One of the greatest crosses we as church leaders will ever carry is that of our own sinfulness, which manifests itself by prying us away from our essential identity in Christ and driving us to seek self-worth in something less than God. For instance, one of the most difficult issues for ministry leaders today is that of negative feedback. I (Steve) can remember any number of times receiving numerous compliments for messages I had presented on Sunday mornings. Multiple people shared how the message as a whole or one particular point or illustration had been used by the Lord to speak some word of encouragement, healing, or challenge into their lives. Yet in the midst of numerous voices of appreciation, one single soul would come forward with a scathing and depreciating comment about the sermon. Many times, the lone critique had absolutely nothing to do with my message at all. I had simply hooked something the individual was struggling with or disliked and I was seen as a safe person to vent their anger upon. At such moments I was tempted to focus exclusively on the isolated criticism rather than seeing it as one small part of a larger picture. It was then that I, like Moses, was tempted to strike the rock.

Managing negative feedback that may not have any firm foundation is one thing. Managing negative feedback that may have some basis in reality is something else altogether. There were quite a few other times when I (Steve) actually made a mistake in what I presented or I came across as hurtful or biased in some manner. I have been corrected for pronunciation mistakes, geographical errors, misquoting the word of God, confused speech, and even occasionally making a word up as I spoke! I suspect many of you can relate. One of the times I remember most vividly was when I told a hilarious true story about a truck driver. The congregation was howling with laughter. Then I ended the account with something like this: "He wasn't a rocket scientist, he was just a truck driver!" Well, you guessed it, sitting right out there in the midst of all those suburbanites was one single truck driver. I had unwittingly and unintentionally hurt a dear brother in Christ by belittling his profession. I truly did need to know of that injury and genuinely apologize for it.

The challenge I faced in the midst of some of those corrections and rebukes was that I would allow them *to preoccupy my mind and heart to the exclusion of the rest of life* that needed to be lived in a faithful way on that particular day. I could have a hundred thankful people on any given

Sunday but my heart would be hijacked by the one critical voice, especially if that criticism was mean-spirited. Like so many persons in church leadership today, I had a tendency to ground my self-worth in the response of those I served rather than in the One I served. A good day equaled a unified good response from the flock.

There is nothing wrong with a good response, for, indeed, we all need confirmation from others to give us the grounding we require to maintain our confidence in our own potency to help shape the world for God's glory. But it is a completely different story to rest deep well-being of soul in public feedback or in ministry measurements such as attendance at worship services or membership numbers. And while all of us are called to be good and trustworthy managers of the things of God (1 Cor 4:2), there are probably going to be years when measurements trend in a negative direction. Sometimes such downward trends are a result of our leadership (and we need to take responsibility for them) and sometimes they have nothing at all to do with us. The point is this: Where am I founding my life? Is it in the applause of the crowd, in pleasing others, in being helpful to the masses, in maintaining my glittering image? Is my self-worth based upon impressive statistical growth in a ministry setting? Or is the foundation of my life being built on something much greater than passing opinion and fleeting praise? Is my definition of self tied up in obediently following the directives of the One who leads me with a gentle yoke and loves me with a steady hand?

Several years ago I read a quote by Mary Lyon (Northumbria Community, 2002) that summarized much of what I am writing about above: "Nine-tenths of our suffering is caused by others not thinking so much of us as we think they ought" (p. 246). Rather than being securely attached to Christ and steady in the face of both the joys and vicissitudes of life, as church leaders we often rise on the waves of good will from others and sink on the ebb of critique or blame from those same people. We experience and pronounce our lives as good when our situational circumstances flow forth with tangible and immediate blessings, but then quickly collapse to despondency when suffering becomes our lot. When we allow self-identity to be largely based upon how useful we are to others (prestige) or how secure we are in building up our own personal empires (power), or the things we hold in our hands or control with our wills (possession and manipulation), then ministry in the name of Jesus rapidly degrades to nothing more than a self-interested and self-directed career. And we become miserable. With St. Augustine (1960), we cry out: "But now, since you lift up him whom you fill with yourself, and since I am not yet filled with you, I am a burden to myself" (p. 255).

Without question Moses was truly a good man. In fact he was one of the great prophets of the Old Testament period. Yet in the fullest understanding of human personhood, he was not a good man who happened to do a few bad deeds. Rather, he was a sinful man who had been touched and called by the Lord his God. Moses stood in as much need of inside-out transformation as any woman or man before or since. In the psalm attributed to his own hand, Moses wrote:

> For we are consumed by your anger;
>> by your wrath we are overwhelmed.
> You have set our iniquities before you,
>> our secret sins in the light of your countenance. (Ps 90:7-8)

The consequences for his angry, disobedient, and untrusting heart were severe. His life mission was not completed. He died outside of the promised land. Because of the corruption of sin, all of us are in danger of a truncated mission short of our life's goal.

Just as Moses was aware of the fading glory of his own countenance, I (Steve), too, am aware that after nearly forty years of serving the church—years filled with some great and high moments, and years containing moments of stumbling in the desert—the glorious presence of the Lord can all too quickly be edged out of life and ministry. Because of falling short "of the glory of God" (Rom 3:23), like Moses I could end up outside of the land of promise. Thus, as I stood on that ancient peak east of the Jordan, I found myself yearning to live in the land of likeness to the Lord and longing for a deepened life of holiness in the Lord. I wanted a life in which grace was allowed to transform the desert of willful sinfulness into a garden of willing responsiveness. I hungered for a heart filled with ever-springing love to bring the grace, light, and goodness of the Lord into the relationships I have with others. I stood alongside Moses, desiring to enter into my heart's homeland. And in the aperture of that awe-filled moment, I sensed in the breezes coming up from the valley below a whispering of invitation to come over into the blessed land of closeness to God. There was within the winds a renewed call to surrender to the purposes of the Lord for my life, ministry, and family, and I discerned a hope that through the sheer graciousness of a loving Redeemer, I, too, could come to the end praying a similar prayer as that of Jesus in John 17:4, "I glorified you on earth by finishing the work that you gave me to do."

# Stepping into the Promise of Transformation

After spending about an hour on Mount Nebo, the group I (Steve) was leading drove down the mountain, across the Jordan River, and into the present-day nation of Israel. Even as we literally entered into the land promised to Moses on that day, I would like for us to consider what it would mean to figuratively enter into the promised land of relational holiness with the Lord and with others. What would be the process of moving from the longing of Mount Nebo into the land of likeness with the Trinity and harmony with the relationships of our lives? Just as I transitioned from one geographical location to another on that day, I do believe there are steps that allow us to be transformed from "one degree of glory to another" (2 Cor 3:18). With great debt to the Christian articulation done by Fr. Adrian van Kaam and Dr. Susan Muto in regard to the ancient Christian path of purgation, illumination, and union, let's look at the royal way of holiness. It is the journey of the soul from spiritual formation through reformation to transformation in Christ.

The infused theological virtues of faith, hope, and love discussed in chapter 1 continue to form, reform, and transform the very structures of our lives through the ongoing threefold process articulated by van Kaam and Muto (2004) of *purifying formation*, *illuminating reformation*, and *unifying transformation*. Let's travel down each of these recurring segments of the path of holiness with the goal in mind of not just eventually arriving but actually living in the land of likeness to our Lord.

# Purifying Formation

Each day of our lives offers many opportunities to either grow in faith, hope, and love, or to allow the deformations of the fall to spread in our spiritual hearts and our relationships with others. Free will gives us an essential choice: we can *willfully* make a decision to allow sin to progress in our lives through giving in to some form of pride, envy, anger, sloth, avarice, lust, or gluttony, or we can *willingly* surrender to a directive of the holy to exercise trust in the goodness of God (faith). In like manner, we can step into a nonanxious confidence in the unfolding purposes of God (hope), or we can allow the debilitating chains of fear and anxiety

45

to stifle our heart. We can then respond with charity to the events in our lives and by doing so embrace our Lord and our neighbor (love), or we can recoil in self-centered preservation and seek to manipulate the events and people we encounter with self-gain in mind. Every day we are moving further into a life that is either in harmony with God, self, and others or that is increasingly discordant with all three.

Directives are continually coming through the events, the persons, even the things of our lives to respond to the challenges posed by each with dependence upon the Lord as expressed through faith, hope, and love. *Consonant* directives are ones that are in accord with the love of God such as when we hear a baby crying and are thereby directed to meet a need of hers. Unfortunately, as a result of the fall, other directives, *dissonant* directives, come as well, directives that do not have the wellspring of the holy as their source. These dissonant directives regularly tempt us to react to the demands of circumstances or the needs of people with prideful self-aggrandizement or anxious retreat rather than self-giving love. In every occasion we are faced with choosing the way of love through saying yes to consonant directives or the route of anxiety, anger, avoidance, or outright sinfulness through implementing dissonant directives. Van Kaam and Muto counsel that discernment is necessary, therefore, to rightly appraise the directives mediated to us through the people, events, and things in our lives. In a thorough discussion of directives in *Dynamics of Spiritual Direction* (2003) they write, "We should distinguish between the many influences that serve the disclosure of our destiny and those that hamper its detection" (p. 40).

Susan came to me, her senior pastor, with a concern from her children's ministry area. Her team arrived at the decision that everyone who taught in any capacity in our children's department should have a statewide fingerprint investigation. Susan's motive was love and protection for the children under her care. It was our discernment that the directives that had moved her and her team were godly and prudent and that she should carry the policy forward.

Susan also had to deal with another directive—fear—that arose from her love for those for whom she was responsible. She was afraid that the policy would be offensive to some of her Sunday school teachers, and this carried with it a sense of anxiety about the situation. She worried that others would react in anger toward her, and she wondered if she might possibly lose some of her teachers. These were legitimate concerns. She anxiously fretted about possible confrontations and negative fallout.

As a minister of the gospel, Susan was not alone in experiencing a certain amount of fear and anxiety over the possible implementation of a ministry requirement for those in her department. She correctly discerned the consonant directives of taking concrete steps to protect the children under her care from predators. Yet, at the same time, she also experienced the dissonant directives of fear over rejection from others and anxiety concerning possible conflict.

The question before Susan was the question that presses each of us as church leaders: *what is really driving the engine of our lives?* Are we motivated toward love and goodwill by the grace and goodness of God that has touched and transformed our lives? Or are we driven by the need to be accepted by those we serve and the fear of inciting conflict with them? Thus, every day multiple directives (consonant and dissonant) arise from situations we face.

Since none of us have escaped collapsing to dissonant directives of one type or another, there is a true need in each of our lives for ongoing repentance (turning from wrong motive and action) and watchfulness at every turn. We desperately need the liturgy of "Confession and Pardon" as found in the *United Methodist Hymnal* that prays:

> Merciful God,
> we confess that we have not loved you with our whole heart.
> We have failed to be an obedient church.
> We have not done your will,
> we have broken your law,
> we have rebelled against your love,
> we have not loved our neighbors,
> and we have not heard the cry of the needy.
> Forgive us, we pray.
> Free us for joyful obedience,
> through Jesus Christ our Lord. Amen. (Young, 1989, p. 12)

The path to spiritual maturity, therefore, travels first through the land of *purifying formation*. When the Holy Spirit warns us that we have allowed an event to trigger fear, anxiety, or any of the deadly sins, right then and there we are handed what needs to be purged from our everyday formation in Christ. As we identify what may literally be squeezing the life out of our hearts with fearful anxiety of something dreadful coming our way, or as we admit to hatred toward someone, or as we sense that we are being misled into the idolatry of placing someone or something other than the Lord as ultimate, or if we allow ourselves to be deceived with the lie that we can provide for our own security and well-being through inordinate work, then the Spirit asks us to be truly sorrowful for such sinfulness and to seek the Lord's gracious mercy to allow us to turn from sin and seek healing.

We very often sense our need for purifying formation because of the conflicts we become embroiled in with others. After working through an excellent process with the stakeholders of her ministry, Susan and her team instituted the policy of a fingerprint background check for every person involved in children's ministry. What ensued was fairly typical of a significant new policy placing additional requirements upon invested parties. The vast majority of teachers and workers saw the good intent behind the policy and realized that the additional layer of security provided to the children would be well worth any inconvenience they, as adults, would briefly experience. On the other hand, a couple of people immediately turned into fiery, outraged critics decrying the injustice of the move and the invasion of their privacy. They were quickly in Susan's face with their anger.

Because of the strength of a right policy, a team solidly behind her, and love for the welfare of all those she served, Susan was able to move through her anxieties concerning conflict and to lovingly yet firmly hold her position with her critics. She allowed purifying formation to turn her away from fear of conflict and personal rejection to a more courageous woman and a stronger, more loving leader. In similar manner the ongoing journey toward spiritual maturity in Christ invites each of us to live in openness to the Spirit's check of any deformative elements in our daily lives. As we become aware of anything contrary to the love of God, faith in Christ, and hope of a transformed life through the Spirit, we allow genuine sorrow over our sinfulness to move our hearts away from darkness and toward the glorious light of the Son of God. Just as a good navigational system provides regular course corrections, purifying formation lifts up the daily "course corrections" we need on our journey home.

# Illuminating Reformation

As we continue upon the path from a land of unlikeness to one of union of likeness with the Trinity, we find that we are quite often surprised by various insights and understandings of the nature of things that open up before us. Like driving around a curve and for the first time beholding a glorious mountain range, the Spirit of God sheds light upon the way as we journey forward. Van Kaam and Muto call this *illuminating reformation* and by it mean "the reception of illuminations pertaining to our life call as hidden in the mind and heart of God" (2004, p. 60). This in-breaking of the light of Christ may come through a particular passage of Scripture, or through prayer. It may arise out of a time of worship or come through a word of spiritual direction. The goodness of God may shine through reading a devotional classic or through the embrace of a loved one. In whatever form it takes, illuminating reformation is a word from the Divine Word who "became flesh and lived among us, and we have seen his glory, the glory as of a father's only son, full of grace and truth. . . . From his fullness we have all received, grace upon grace" (John 1:14, 16).

These illuminating moments are gifts of divine love. They come in response to hearts that are hungry for righteousness and committed to following the one who named himself as "the way, and the truth, and the life" (John 14:6). They are at one and the same time an embrace of heavenly love, a sign of eternal forgiveness, an evidence of the faith that God has in us, and a hope-filled confirmation that God is indeed showing us "the path of life" (Ps 16:11). They are also invitations to obedience, calling us to love whatever directive has been given and to step into (incarnate) the action called for. As we turn away from behaviors that, as Toddy will put it in chapter 6, are more jerklike than Christlike, our lives begin undergoing major reconstruction. This wonderful *reformation* of heart and actions unfolds as we follow the light we have received from the Lord.

In his second letter to the Corinthian church, Saint Paul gives us a strategic view of the process of illuminating reformation when he writes of the "greater glory" (2 Cor 3:10) or shining presence of the holy that has come through Christ. It is greater in the sense that it is the fulfillment of the law that was handed to humanity through Moses. And it is glorious in the sense that Jesus the Christ has ushered in a ministry of justification, not condemnation, that abounds in the very presence of the light and goodness of God (2 Cor 3:9).

Paul is clearly communicating that this new, permanent glory that has come in and through the person and work of Christ does not have to gradually fade away in our lives, as did the glow from Moses' face. While not denying long walks in desert spaces, Paul is affirming that as we continue to turn to the Lord through purifying formation, the "veil" of hardness of heart and mind is removed (2 Cor 3:16). Then Paul breaks forth with these transformational verses:

> Now the Lord is the Spirit, and where the Spirit of the Lord is, there is freedom. And all of us, with unveiled faces, seeing the glory of the Lord as though reflected in a mirror, are being transformed into the same image from one degree of glory to another; for this comes from the Lord, the Spirit. (2 Cor 3:17-18)

When we turn from striking rocks and people in anger over our desert pilgrimage, we are not just turning away from discordance. It takes much more than any self-help method that only stresses letting go of the negative! We turn away from personal evil and in so doing we turn toward the fair light of Jesus. It is in this turning *toward* that brings us to gaze upon a magnificent presence of light and life that is the glory of God.

For Paul, there is literally a process of re-creation going on. Something new came in Christ and something new was transpiring in the hearts of believers. Just as light was created in the first chapter of Genesis to give definition to what was formerly under darkness, now the Lord is completely remaking those who want to know the light of God's love. The key word is "seeing" (2 Cor 3:18), which means not just to passively glance at something but to truly behold or to contemplate what is seen. Paul is affirming that as we lovingly behold the glorious presence of the Lord Jesus Christ and allow the magnitude of his person to settle into our hearts, then the unheard of begins to actually transpire. Old men and women *are* radically transformed into something new (John 3:4), and anyone, young or old, who lovingly gazes upon the person of Christ and allows his radiance to form and reform their life becomes "a new creation: everything old has passed away; see, everything has become new!" (2 Cor 5:17).

Psalm 50:1-2 proclaims:

> The mighty one, God the LORD,
> speaks and summons the earth
> from the rising of the sun to its setting.
> Out of Zion, the perfection of beauty,
> God shines forth.

In beholding the "perfection of beauty" which is the shining presence of God, Paul says this: we (the church) become transformed into the same image. That is, we take on the same nature as the Lord himself. And this process, according to the original Greek text, moves forward from "glory to glory." Whether Paul meant moving from the old glory of the law into the new permanent glory of the Son, or moving successively by stages into the presence and nature of Christ, either way points to the same reality. As we contemplate the person of the Lord, we are moved into the promised land of likeness to the Lord. And it is not our doing at all! It comes only through the loving, transformational power of the Spirit of God who reconstructs us in the image and nature of the Son.

In his masterful text on discipleship, *The Divine Conspiracy: Rediscovering Our Hidden Life in God*, Dallas Willard presses the question and process of "how to bring God adequately before the mind of the disciple" (1998, p. 324). In seeking to establish "A Curriculum for Christlikeness," Willard writes:

> This is to be done in such a way that love for and delight in God will be elicited and established as the pervasive orientation of the whole self. It will fill the mind of the willing soul and progress toward an easy and delightful governance of the entire personality. (p. 324)

Indeed, Jesus taught, "Everyone then who hears these words of mine and acts on them will be like a wise man who built his house on rock" (Matt 7:24). The very nature of discipleship implies "one who follows another." Saint Paul follows through with the practical application of a curriculum for spiritual maturity that will result in relational holiness. In 2 Corinthians 3, Paul offers us the curriculum of loving focus upon the person of Jesus.

Willard (1998) explains that

> the assumption of Jesus' program for his people on earth was that they would live their lives as his students and co-laborers. They would find him so admirable in every respect—wise, beautiful, powerful, and good—that they would constantly seek to be in his presence and be guided, instructed, and helped by him in every aspect of their lives. For he is indeed the living head of the community of prayerful love across all time and space. (p. 273)

Today we seek to be in his presence by gazing upon his form. Our turning to the Lord and seeing his glory helps provide the open door through which the Spirit can bring the grace of illuminating reformation. Such turning always implies following. The early church father, Gregory of Nyssa (1978) reminds us that "to follow God wherever he might lead is to behold God" (p. 119).

How does this work? And how can we formatively behold the Son of God? Certainly there is not one standard answer or any uniform method to enable us to contemplate the beauty of Christ. Entire schools of thought have arisen to seek to provide a way for adherents of the gospel to fully follow the way of the Son. Technique is not the issue. What we are after is loving attention to the revelation of Christ in whatever consonant manner that can come to individuals and to communities of faith. Suffice it to say, in its simplest form we can formatively keep the person of Jesus before our hearts and minds through the showings we have of him in the Gospels.

Let's just take a few examples from the inexhaustible resource of the Gospels. As we behold Jesus welcoming and blessing the little children in Mark 10:13-16, we see one who had a gentle and loving spirit. He deeply valued the children and saw them as persons of worth that could even teach their adult supervisors an important lesson about trust, openness, and the kingdom of God. Just as he demonstrated a wonderful balance between gentleness and firmness in that encounter, we open our lives to the same patience, kindness, and gentleness with which he loved the children around him. We also allow him to give us the courage to be lovingly firm with those who stratify society by cutting out or devaluing entire segments of humanity.

When through grace we are enabled to turn from our hardness of heart, we can also live out the simple example of sweetness and gentleness in our Lord toward all vulnerable people. With his compassion we take up the children in our lives in arms of loving protection and we share with them the confident benediction of God's goodness. Then, without any malice that would seek to punish others, we allow the fortitude and truth of this Jesus whom we adore to strengthen our love and impart his courage to stand against anything that excludes benediction from others. And when our stand of love necessitates firmness, we do so seeking the highest good of those we must counter.

For most of us in the press of ministry, it is imperative that we behold the person of Christ in the midst of stressful, demanding settings where anxiety is high and anger is flaring between individuals. We see such a setting in Luke 10:38-42. In this encounter in Martha's home we read that she extended an exceptionally gracious invitation to Jesus and his disciples. It would be gracious in any age to invite a dozen or more men into your home, but in a time of no refrigeration, running water, or electrical appliances of any kind, this was truly an extraordinary act of love.

Here is the setting Luke records: The invited guests come in and everyone, including Martha's sister, Mary, gather around Jesus to hear him share; everyone, that is, but Martha. Poor Martha was left in the kitchen by herself to do all of the work while her sister lazily lounged at the feet of the Master. No doubt, Martha's anger with her sister magnified even as her anxiety built over the impossibility of getting supper ready at a decent hour. Finally, enough was enough and she stormed out of the kitchen and protested, "Lord, do you not care that my sister has left me to do all the work by myself? Tell her then to help me" (Luke 10:40). Just imagine a fiery-mad, anxiety-ridden woman making such a demand to the Son of God!

When "our name is Martha" and the situation before us seems both intolerable and impossible as it was when Jesus was invited to her home, we can behold the grace of God with the same calming words of priority and love. With the compassion of Eternity, Jesus names the trouble: "Martha, your sister is not the issue. You have allowed your heart to become agitated and resentful because you are internally divided over all you have to do. But, dear Martha, your sister is actually showing you the way of life." We behold the calming word of priority: "One thing is needful" (KJV). Loving attention upon the Son of God will always remain the greatest priority of our lives. Get this priority in place and the seeming overwhelming tasks of life fall into their proper place in due time. But if we miss this priority, then the sin of Martha's anxiety, which prevented her from seeing the grace of the moment and resulted in the tragedy of resentment that drove a wedge between her and her sister, will be ours as well. What we see is the glory of divine love that unites a scattered heart by giving it a single purpose. And what we witness is the persuasion of love that guards against venting unnecessary anxiety against others. Such singleness of heart and gifting of love is imparted as grace upon grace from the one who visits in our homes.

We become what we behold. We are transformed into what we say yes to. The reforming, restructuring grace of Trinitarian love comes through loving attention and heartfelt gazing upon the beauty and winsomeness of Jesus. Whether we affix the gaze of our affectionate hearts on the parables, the stories, the accounts, or the teachings of Jesus, or we enter into the cloud of unknowing and expect to meet the mystery of God beyond any visual image our minds are given, we are being encountered by the light of the holy. And our lives are not left the same after such epiphanies.

# Unifying Transformation

Through the process of purifying formation the Holy Spirit brings to mind those deformative areas in our lives that are not in harmony with our Lord and with others. The purifying fire of God's love reveals the impact of original sin and the deformity it has left in our hearts. As we exhibit heartfelt remorse over our dissimilarity to the God we love, we are enabled through the mercy of God to turn away from hardness of heart as well as from attitudes and actions that have had a detrimental impact upon others. In our need for forgiveness and restoration of damaged relationships, we find ourselves receptive to whatever word the Lord chooses to share with us. Then, as we act upon the specific light of God's word that has been imparted, the sheer grace of God not only reorders our interior, but also actually imparts divine virtue that simply was not present before. The goodness of God's love does for us what no amount of self-help could ever do. It builds a whole new self.

In describing the spiritual movement of unifying transformation, van Kaam and Muto (2004) write:

> Our actual life form may still be fragmented; its remodeling by grace may be less than we might desire, yet grace continues to move us to model and mirror Christ. Transfiguration in him marks the crowning point of our life's unfolding. Here on earth this graced striving may recast our character and personality. Under the guidance of God, the divine stream of our Christian existence may reach that final acceleration which will draw us, as it did the Apostle Paul, beyond the veils of time into spousal union with the Eternal. (p. 61)

Spiritual maturity then is not difficult to understand at all. It is nothing less than modeling and mirroring Christ. It is keeping the light of the Lord Jesus Christ before us and allowing that light to radically transform our entire existence. John Wesley (1966) used the terms "entire sanctification" or "Christian perfection" and described it this way: "Scripture perfection is pure love filling the heart, and governing all the words and actions" (p. 60).

Wesleyan theologian Kenneth Collins (2007) writes:

> Entire sanctification not only entails actual renewal, transformation, and purification through the ever-potent grace of God, but also marks a genuine healing of the soul. . . . Christian perfection entails the freedom, now graciously restored, to obey the two great commandments of which Jesus spoke, to "love the Lord your God with all your heart, and with all your soul, and with all your mind . . . And a second . . . you shall love your neighbor as yourself" (Matt 22:37-39). . . .
>
> Entire sanctification, then, is love replacing sin, holy love conquering every vile passion and temper. It not only includes a "heart and life all devoted to God," but also embraces the purification of the *relation* between God and humanity such that the *imago Dei*, especially the moral image, has been renewed in its glory and splendor. The creature, once steeped in sin, now reflects the goodness of the Creator in a remarkable way. Being properly related to the Most High, believers give evidence of the divine glory that shines through their being. Christian perfection, then, is another term for holy love. . . . "Blessed be God," Wesley exclaims, " . . . we know there is nothing deeper, there is nothing better in heaven or earth than the God of love!" (p. 302)

The process of moving from purifying formation through illuminating reformation to unifying transformation is the royal path of holiness of heart and life. When we stay on this path as a community of believers, we come to what Paul described as "the unity of the faith and of the knowledge of the Son of God, to maturity, to the measure of the full stature of Christ" (Eph 4:13). We are transformed into God's church, even the body of Christ.

# The Mount of Transformation

I can only speculate but I believe that Moses died on Mount Nebo with an almost unfathomable desire for the Lord burning within his heart. That transition very well could have been as Gregory of Nyssa (1979) reflected about Moses, "Though raised to such heights, he is still restless with desire, is more and more dissatisfied, and still thirsts for that which had filled him to capacity" (p. 145). For the "true vision of God," according to Gregory of Nyssa, "consists rather in this, that the soul that looks up to God never ceases to desire Him" (p. 146).

The next glimpse of Moses we are given comes in Matthew 17:3 when he, along with Elijah, appears before the three disciples and Jesus on the

Mount of Transfiguration. Moses did get to go into the land after all! He was ushered into the land of likeness with the Trinity and was able to talk with the Lord face-to-face once again. The vision of entering into a land where sin is separated from the soul and we are enabled to grow in grace and, "in the knowledge of Christ, in the love and image of God; and will do so, not only till death, but to all eternity" (Wesley, 1966, p. 62) is the vision of relational holiness and spiritual maturity before God's church today.

# CHAPTER FOUR

# RELATIONAL HOLINESS: EMOTIONAL MATURITY

*Instead, speaking the truth in love, we will in all things grow up into him who is the Head, that is, Christ.—Ephesians 4:15 NIV*

Church leaders do not wake up one morning and find that they have somehow lost their soul for ministry in the same way that they may have lost their car keys. Losing heart only *appears* to come out of the blue. In actuality warning signs exist that can alert church leaders to the reality that they are dancing on the edge of a slippery slope. For example, a slow but steady erosion of personal boundaries is a forewarning of trouble. Boundaries tell the difference between my things and your things, my space and your space. Some boundaries are visible, like fences around one's property. Other boundaries are invisible, such as those around your heart. Boundaries also vary in the degree to which they are opened or closed to others, or their degree of permeability. An open boundary says "y'all come." A closed boundary says "no admittance." Permeable boundaries allow some people to come closer and they keep others farther away. When the demands of stuck-togetherness are greater than one's ability to maintain individuality, then a person might emotionally fuse with the person who is making the stuck-togetherness demands. This is an example of the near-disappearance of an emotional boundary. Conversely, a person might use cutoff to revolt and resist the demands for stuck-togetherness. This is an example of slamming one's boundaries shut.[1]

Jesus' boundaries surprised people. He claimed an intimacy with God that was unknown to the Jewish community of his day. He drew those who were marginalized in his society closer to him while he kept the religious elite at arm's length. He called a motley group of twelve men to be with him (Mark 3:14), and the gospel writers report that even among this select group he invited three (Peter, James, and John) to step closer. Jesus' boundaries included clarity and certainty about his mission on earth. For example, Jesus "had to go" through Samaria (John 4:4) when others would intentionally go around Samaria. He ignored the Jewish social markers that declared who was "in" and who was "out" of the kingdom of God, in spite of pressure by the Scribes and Pharisees that Jesus conform to the social conventions of his day (i.e., Jesus ate with sinners, conversed with women, honored children, and healed on the Sabbath).

How was Jesus able to maintain such clear boundaries? One could argue that being the Son of God was a big boost to having strong boundaries. While that may be true, Jesus also knew *who* he was, *whose* he was, and *what* he was about (John 13:1-5). He was clear about what beliefs and values were the foundation of his life and he lived in a way that was consistent with these guiding foundations *even when others were pressuring him to change* (Mark 8:31-38; 14:43-50). Jesus knew when others were anxious (Mark 1: 35-38; 2:23-28) but he did not get caught up in their anxiety. Quite the contrary, Jesus' own sense of calm assurance quieted the hearts of many, such as his own disciples (Mark 4:35-41; 6:30-52). He claimed responsibility for his own life (John 10:14-19) and he acted responsibly toward others.

How well do you tend to your boundaries? In order to rightly adjust your boundaries, you need to know where they are and how to maintain them under stressful situations. Managing your boundaries is essential if you are to keep your passion for church leadership, and it's most challenging when you are in the midst of an anxious group of parishioners. Family systems theory refers to the ability to wisely manage one's boundaries as the capacity for a *differentiated self* (White and Center, 2002). As you read the following vignette, reflect on how Royce handled his boundaries.

# Royce's Story

Royce left a successful career in business to follow God's call to preach the word.[2] Upon his completion of Bible college, he became the associate pastor in a thriving suburban church. Royce was involved in some aspect of ministry from dawn to dusk. It had been weeks since he had taken his day off. But he didn't mind. There was no end to the peoples' needs, and Royce believed it was his responsibility to meet all of them. After all, this was God's call on his life.

Unfortunately, this approach to ministry came with a price. Royce was so busy doing God's work that he had little time to deepen his relationship with God, his family, or his close relationships with a few friends. The harder Royce worked, the more sensitive he became to criticism. And the longer he worked, the more susceptible he became to haunting feelings of inadequacy. His solution to self-doubt was to work harder and longer. He felt like he had over 350 bosses, and no matter how hard he tried, somebody was unhappy with him. Royce could not tolerate this, as he became distraught whenever someone was mad at him. Subsequently he became obsessed with making sure that everybody liked him and that all approved of his ministry.

Naturally, Royce turned to his wife, Ashley, for emotional support. Throughout his business career, Ashley had been his rock, his shelter in the stormy blast. He relied on her to build him up when he was down, and to comfort him when he was anxious. She was the foundation upon which he stood emotionally. The previous level of support that Ashley gave Royce now seemed like a drop of water in an ocean of insecurity. It wasn't that she said *nothing* about his church leadership. It was just that what she said was not what Royce wanted to hear. Instead of *exclusively* praising him, she sometimes offered critiques. This was not to Royce's liking. A slow but steady distance developed in their once-intimate relationship. Unfortunately, Royce and Ashley were so focused on what they were doing for God that they were oblivious to what was happening to them.

Then along came Mary. Mary was the church's administrative assistant. She worked closely with Royce on a daily basis, helping him with the myriad details that accompanied his pastoral responsibilities. Royce found great solace in Mary's presence. When he was with her, he discovered that he felt better about himself and his leadership. In addition, he looked forward to her handwritten notes of affirmation. At first he shared these notes with Ashley, but he stopped doing so when Ashley began to question the nature of his relationship with Mary. Royce thought that Ashley was overreacting. Mary was his ministry colleague and she understood the strains of ministry in a way that Ashley didn't.

One day, Royce realized that the hugs that he gave Mary were more than a display of brotherly affection. Royce began to entertain the idea of getting physically closer to Mary. He realized that he would be violating his marriage vows, but after all, what harm would one time do? He was only a little associate pastor in an unimportant church. No one would ever find out.[3] After three years of an on-again, off-again affair, Royce realized that this secret relationship no longer provided the perks that it had in the beginning. He wanted out. He knew that what he had done was sinful and his sin was getting heavy. Then he thought about the "geographic cure." He would seek another pastorate. In Royce's mind that would give him a clean break and a fresh start.

# What's Up with Royce?

Royce seeks an "accountability-free" escape. However, a pain-free way out of this sinful mess does not exist. If his affair is discovered, the best possible outcome includes Royce's confession and repentance, and his commitment to the restoration of his marriage, assuming that Amanda will take him back (Holeman, 2004). This also opens the door for Mary to access advocacy, healing, and counseling.[4] In some contexts, Royce would forfeit his right to pastor and would surrender his ordination papers. In other church settings, Royce would be required to go through a structured process of restoration before he could resume the pulpit again. In our opinion, the worst possible outcome would be for this sin to remain secret, generating a strong undertow of anxiety that would trouble the waters of these three families (i.e., Royce/Ashley, Mary, and the church family) for years to come.

What observations can we make about Royce's boundaries? Perhaps you noticed that Royce failed to care for himself when he worked nonstop. Or maybe you saw that Royce failed to protect the sanctity of his marriage. These are indeed boundary violations. But what sense do you make about Royce's perception that he was responsible for meeting everybody's needs (taking over/overfunctioning)? Or his overwhelming concern that others accept and approve of him (emotional fusion)? Or his excessive reliance on Ashley, and then Mary, to shore up his flagging self-esteem (giving over/underfunctioning)? Or his use of distance to manage his marital conflict? Or his desire to evade personal accountability with the geographic cure (withdrawing/cutoff)? These are examples of gridlock and the two-choice dilemma (see chapter 2) in Royce's life. The kind of anxiety associated with gridlock contributes to the erosion of personal boundaries in church leadership and interferes with one's growth in spiritual maturity (see chapter 3).

That's the bad news. Now the good news. This crisis can become the catalyst for spiritual, emotional, and interpersonal maturity or growth in relational holiness. You may recall that in chapter 1 we suggested spiritual, emotional, and interpersonal maturity were important components of relational holiness. In chapter 2 we described how unchecked anxiety can undermine one's desire to go on to maturity. In chapter 3 we explored some contours of spiritual maturity. We saw how drawing closer to God equips church leaders to access the power of the Holy Spirit so that leaders may live as exemplars of personal and social holiness.

In this chapter we turn our attention to yet another aspect of relational holiness, that is, emotional maturity. Here you will learn about three central elements of emotional maturity: differentiation of self, self-soothing, and self-responsibility.[5] This focus on self may be alarming to some, as these concepts are often confused with selfishness and self-centeredness. However, without a firm sense of *who* one is and *whose* one is—without a clear sense of self—a church leader is susceptible to the whims of everyone around her. Without the ability to calm one's own anxiety, a leader will look to other people or things to do that for him like Royce did. And without taking ownership of the consequences of one's actions, a leader will seek scapegoats to carry the blame.

# Differentiation of Self

"Differentiation of self" is a fifty-cent psychological phrase that has important implications for church leaders. Clearly you won't locate this phrase in the pages of holy writ. Nevertheless, you will find that individuals in Scripture, including our Lord Jesus Christ, embodied it. We'll start with its biblical and theological counterparts, and then we will move our discussion to how this applies to church leaders.

Differentiation is a concept that theologians such as Jürgen Moltmann (1981), Wolfhart Pannenberg (1991), and Stanley Grenz (2001) have applied to the Trinity. According to Grenz, the Trinity is "a community and fellowship among three equal persons" (p. 45). The members of the Godhead are complete persons who are intimately connected with one another, and yet who are also distinguishable from one another. They are selves and they are persons-in-relationship. The term *perichoresis* describes a divine dance of relationality, in which each member of the Trinity *must be fully present* for the dance to be complete. The rhythm of the dance emanates from the self-giving, other-directed love that flows between the members of the Godhead. When the Father loves the Son, this love does not diminish the Father. When the Son gives the Holy Spirit, there is not less of the Son than there had been before the Spirit was given. When the Spirit glorifies the Father and the Son, the Spirit does not lose anything. The relationship among the persons of the Trinity perfectly models *intimate connection and individuality* without the demands for stuck-togetherness as Murray Bowen defined it (Kerr and Bowen, 1988).

Differentiation is not about individualism. It is about individuals in close relationships with others. Differentiation of self is the capacity to connect with others *while maintaining one's individuality*. Or said differently, it is the capacity to maintain one's individuality *when communing with others*. As modeled by the Trinity, relationships founded upon differentiation require each party to bring a full self to the fellowship table.

From a family-systems perspective, Peter Titelman (2003) suggests that differentiation of self is "the ability to act for oneself without being selfish and the ability to act for others without being selfless" (p. 20). Edwin Friedman (1985) defines differentiation of self as the capacity

> to define [one's] own life's goals and values apart from surrounding [stuck-togetherness] pressures, to say "I" when others are demanding "you" and "we." It includes the capacity to maintain a (relatively) nonanxious presence in the midst of anxious systems, to take maximum responsibility for one's own destiny and emotional being. It can be measured somewhat by the breadth of one's repertoire of responses when confronted with crisis. . . . *Differentiation means the capacity to be an "I" while remaining connected.* (p. 27, emphasis added)

The portrait of differentiation of self was first painted by innovative family therapist Murray Bowen in the late twentieth century. Bowen hypothesized that one could arrange individuals along a scale of differentiation. Some people functioned at higher levels of differentiation and others functioned at lower levels. Bowen believed that most adults were in the mid-range of the scale. One's adult level of differentiation was determined during childhood by the way parents responded to the child's desire for individuality in relationship to the family's demand for togetherness, or stuck-togetherness in more dysfunctional families. Bowen was pessimistic about the degree to which one could increase one's level of differentiation in adulthood, although he did believe that people could make small but important increases in differentiation with hard work. Because we believe that with Jesus Christ *all things are possible*, we also believe that one can experience significant changes in one's level of differentiation through the power of the Holy Spirit and the love of the community of believers.

What does differentiation of self look like in action? In the next section we will discuss five components of differentiation: a clear picture of who you are in relation to others, the ability to tell the difference between your thinking and your feeling, a lack of fear about relationship engulfment or abandonment, a robust repertoire of ways to respond to others, and a tolerance of pain for the sake of growth. Subsequent sections of this chapter will deal with two additional characteristics of differentiation, that is, the ability to self-soothe and maintain a nonanxious presence, and the willingness to take maximum responsibility for the impact of one's words and actions.

First, when you are an "I," you know who you are, what you believe, and you have thought through your life goals. You are able to manifest these basic commitments in your interactions with others so your walk matches your talk. Your beliefs can, and should, include your theological commitments and how your life manifests these theological beliefs. Ronald Richardson (1996) observes that "we may have essentially 'correct beliefs,' but without the ability to be more differentiated, we will not be able to act consistently on these beliefs. The better differentiated we are, the more we can behave in ways consistent with our professed beliefs" (p. 182). If we refer to Royce for a moment, we could suppose that Royce affirmed marital fidelity and possibly even preached about it, but at a particular moment in time he did not live his life consistent with that belief. Richardson would suggest that this disconnect between Royce's walk and talk is partially due to his lack of differentiation.

Contra Frank Sinatra, differentiation of self is not exclusively about doing things "my way." That is more akin to rugged individualism. Conversely, the aspect of *individuation* that comes into play is clarity about who you are *when you must choose* this way or that, especially when others are pressuring you to conform to their expectations, desires, dreams, or wants in ways that would compromise you (i.e., violate your beliefs and values). This is not as clear-cut as it may seem. Drawing the proverbial line in the sand, or maintaining one's boundaries through differentiation, comes into focus *when others are pressuring you to be different*, when *they* are anxious and they want you to change to make *them* more comfortable, and when an undesired consequence may come your way if your choose to maintain your integrity instead of giving in to relationship anxiety. You may have experienced this in your youth when peers demanded that you conform to their image of who you should be if you wanted to maintain a relationship with them. Or you may have experienced this with your parents when they demanded that you conform to their image of who you should be if you wanted to remain in their good graces.

Contra popular culture, differentiation of self is also not about "my way or the highway," a "like it or lump it" approach to life. This style implies that you will leave the relationship unless the other person goes along with your demands. Differentiation is about the *harder* task of remaining true to who God has called you to be *and* staying appropriately connected to others. An example of this might be remaining friends with a husband and wife who are divorcing. You do not have to choose sides. You cannot control whether either the husband or wife makes side-taking *a condition of his or her* remaining friends with you. You may indeed lose the friendship of one of them if you continue to relate to both of them. The important point here is that you do not lose a part of your self because you caved into a demand that was against your principles. It is the other person's choice to stay or leave at that point.

In other words, individuals who maintain a solid sense of self know what they think, want, and value, and they are able to let others have their own thoughts, feelings, and desires without feeling threatened ("They must agree with me") or diminished ("I feel inadequate if you disagree with me. You must be right and I must be wrong"). This does not imply that you are closed to the influence of others. Well-defined leaders are able to hear others' viewpoints and to thoughtfully consider their validity. Because they are secure, differentiated leaders do not lose face when they change their minds. They can admit when they are wrong without being flooded with shame.

Second, when you are an "I," you are able to distinguish your thinking from your feelings, and you can determine which of these important functions to call upon during any interpersonal exchange. During difficult conversations, differentiated church leaders manage their emotional intensity in such a way that their emotional brain system does not hijack their thinking brain system (see chapter 2). According to family therapist Roberta M. Gilbert (1992),

> at higher levels of differentiation . . . people have more choice about whether to follow the guidance of the thinking self or the guidance of the emotional/feeling self. . . . At lower levels of differentiation, the intellectual and emotional guidance systems are fused, allowing little or no choice between the two and making the intellect essentially emotionally driven. (p. 21)

This does not mean that you turn yourself into a sanctified version of a talking head—all thinking and no feeling. Such was Mr. Spock, a character from the original Star Trek series who was known for his exclusive use of logic to solve interpersonal problems. Mr. Spock *had* emotions, but he treated them with disdain as he believed that they served no useful purpose. This is not differentiation. Leaders can be—and should be—passionate about what they believe as well as the vision that they have for their church. Some differentiated leaders could be labeled as intense people (consider the Apostle Paul, for example). What distinguishes emotionally driven undifferentiated leadership from passionate and differentiated leadership is the degree to which the leader can be connected to others who disagree. Differentiated leaders are able to maintain their position and *invite* the other to join them without resorting to manipulation or coercion. In addition, they are willing to let the other leave. That separation may bring sadness, even disappointment, but it will not bring about personal devastation.

We fully acknowledge and want to be sensitive to the fact that an inordinate number of parishioners in today's society opt to leave their church settings. Reasons for this exodus vary from the ridiculous (we don't like the fact that this preacher gives us outlines in the bulletin and asks us to take notes from her sermons) to the tragic (this pastor simply doesn't care about us) to everything in between. When a beloved parishioner walks away from his church home, a sense of loss and sorrow comes into our hearts. What we are suggesting is that a spiritually mature, differentiated church leader will acknowledge the loss, and will even be able to absorb the inevitable anger that will come from others within the congregation over the departure of a family member without absorbing a debilitating sense of shame or blame. Sometimes, after doing all that we can lovingly do, people make the decision to leave our flock. A differentiated leader blesses the exiting person while maintaining personal stability in leadership.

Third, when you are an "I," you fear neither engulfment nor abandonment. In other words, when you have a solid sense of self you are not vigilant about whether or not someone or even a congregation will swallow you whole or spit you out. This is because you maintain your own boundaries in terms of closeness and distance. Family therapist Philip Guerin and his colleagues (1996) observe that fear of engulfment or abandonment is the foundation for much of our relationship anxiety. In church leaders this fear may show up as an "inordinate concern over being loved and accepted, which may take the form of worrying about what people think of them or the opposite—rebelling against accepted behavior or standards" (Gilbert, 1992, p. 25).

Both of us have counseled any number of church leaders who struggled with this particular aspect of differentiation. They believed that *everyone should like them.* The reality is that it is impossible to be an effective leader without saying no at appropriate times. That is part of the leader's responsibility. However, few people like hearing no, and immature, less differentiated individuals may go away mad, and even threaten to leave the church. If the church leader is not able to calm his anxiety when somebody is upset, then that leader will be immobilized when he has to make an unpopular, but necessary, decision. Such a leader will set about the totally impossible task of seeking to please everyone, or even worse, trying to please the most influential persons within the congregational setting.

Pioneer family therapist Murray Bowen (Kerr and Bowen, 1988) also saw these two fears as signs of lower levels of differentiation. Fear of abandonment eventually drove people to stick to others as if they were emotionally fused together. Behind this desperate need for contact was the belief that I would somehow emotionally wither and perish if others distanced themselves from me. Participants in fused relationships sought to stay attached to others at all costs. The image of an emotional leech is not too far from reality. When someone fuses with another, he spends his time thinking about how the other will react, that is, he thinks, feels, and plans more around the other person than around the self. Fear of engulfment can be expressed as distancing behaviors, in its milder guise, or as emotional cutoff, in its extreme form. When people use cutoff, they use physical or emotional distance to keep themselves calm. Cutoff should not be confused with taking an emotional time-out. Cutoff is an automatic, knee-jerk reaction to anxiety. A time-out, on the other hand, is a thoughtful, chosen response that one makes in order to regain emotional control *so that* one can stay engaged and connected.

Fears of abandonment and engulfment set the stage for the pursuer/distancer dance. We react to our fear of abandonment by pursuing others. This pursuit can take three forms. First, this can take the form of our using guilt or shame to motivate the other person to stay close to us. The following dialogue is an example of this:

> Committee member: I need to resign from this committee as my family situation has changed.
>
> Committee leader: I can't believe that you are saying this! You are the only person who can fill this role. Are you sure you have prayed about this?

Can you feel the implicit guilt and shame message in the committee leader's response? While some people can be controlled by guilt and shame, others will respond by moving away from the one who uses these recruitment tactics.

Second, it can take the form of taking over the relationship by being highly directive. The fear behind this is that if others are given the option to decide for themselves, they may not stay connected to you. Family therapist Edwin Friedman (1985) notes that leaders with lower levels of differentiation are reactive when others distance from them. Leaders with higher levels of differentiation remain calm when others emotionally pull away. In these moments, secure church leaders open their ears to listen to why others are distancing instead of trying to teach them why they should remain close.

Third, we react to our fear of engulfment by pushing others away. This can also take different forms. The distancing church leader is impossible to reach, delays making important decisions, agrees to a course of action but fails to follow through. The leader may also use anger to push others away. Leaders with higher levels of differentiation remain calm when others ask for more closeness. More differentiated leaders evaluate whether the request is reasonable. For example, a parishioner may ask her pastor to disciple her. This is a reasonable request and the differentiated leader will be sure that the appointments are held at times and places that protects both of them from boundary violations.[6]

Fourth, when you are an "I," you are not locked into knee-jerk reactions when responding to others. You are clear about your life principles and are able to match your walk to your talk. You are able to think more clearly, objectively, and neutrally about situations and interactions that evoke anxiety within you. You are also able to imagine a number of optional responses to these situations, and the most likely consequences of these options. This gives you the ability to act flexibly within a given situation based on your relatively objective assessment. Developing more flexibility in relationships requires several things. First, we need to expand our awareness of how we think, feel, and act when we interact with another. Second, we need to examine our attitude about the relationship to see if we are blaming the other or harboring immature expectations. Finally, we need to think through our options (Klever, 2003). For example, I (Toddy) have learned that my level of differentiation slips when I am trying to keep too many balls in the air. At these times, my knee-jerk response to most new requests is no. When I catch myself doing this, I have learned to slow down and take time to *think* about the request, *evaluate* its relative merits and costs, and *then* reply. I have been known to change a no into a yes in hindsight.

Fifth, when you are an "I," you are able to tolerate pain for the sake of growth (Friedman, 1985; Schnarch, 1997, 2002). The pain in leadership comes in numerous forms. One type of pain is the pain of persistence in the face of crisis. About this, Dan Allender (2006), founder and president of Mars Hill Graduate School, writes:

> A requirement of leadership is that we operate at high levels of intensity for lengthy periods of time. The battering waves of crisis don't stop, and often the structures that are designed to move us forward break down under constant friction. One breakdown usually exposes the weakness in the process, people, and systems. And new crises are birthed in the face of precipitating crisis. (p. 45)

Because a person with a solid sense of self has clarity about her goals, she steers her team through these storms of crises with minimal wavering.

A second type of pain in leadership comes from interactions with others who refuse to mature in Christ, with those who prefer to take over, give over, or withdraw. While it would be nice if others would change, the purpose of differentiation is to improve *one's own emotional functioning. It is not about changing others!* To be sure, as a church leader works to clarify his position and as he remains relatively calm when anxiety increases, others will be challenged to do the same. Unfortunately, they may not embrace the opportunity to grow.

How does the concept of differentiation of self fit with Christ's call for self-denial found in Luke 9:23-25?

> Whoever wants to be my disciple must deny themselves and take up their cross daily and follow me. For whoever wants to save their life will lose it, but whoever loses their life for me will save it. What good is it for you to gain the whole world, and yet lose or forfeit your very self? (TNIV)

And in Philippians 2:5-7:

> In your relationships with one another, have the same attitude of mind Christ Jesus had: Who, being in very nature God, / did not consider equality with God something to be used to his own advantage; / rather, he made himself nothing / by taking the very nature of a servant, / being made in human likeness. (TNIV)

Clearly, from these passages, a Christ-centered life of self-denial stands in stark contrast to selfishness and self-centeredness. Selfish church leaders take little consideration for others. They are most concerned with their own needs, comfort, and promotion. Selfish leaders *use* the stuck-togetherness force to get what they want or to keep what they have. Self-centered leaders expect others to meet their needs no matter what it might cost the other person. Self-centered church leaders also have an exaggerated sense of their own importance and a callous disregard for the impact of their behaviors on others. Self-differentiated leadership does not require one to inflate one's own importance through self-promotion nor to deflate the importance of others for self-protection. As Ronald Richardson (1996) observes:

> Self-centeredness is the failure to achieve this greater objectivity; it is subjective and keeps us at the center of what is happening, as if the purpose of life is all about us. And selfishness includes wanting others to be the way we want them to be; it does not respect the individuality of others. (p. 177)

Because self-differentiated church leaders are secure in their identity in Christ, they are able to joyfully sacrifice for the sake of others *because* they *choose* to give out of love rather than give begrudgingly to another only out of a sense of duty. Servant leadership replaces selfish leadership goals, and *kenotic* love (the "self-emptying" of Jesus described in Philippians 2:7) marks our heart and ministry.

Self-denial is often confused with the idea of self-annihilation in our churches. Here we need to make a distinction between giving ourselves completely to Christ (as Steve discussed in chapter 3) and giving ourselves over to another fallible human being. When I give myself to Christ, I actually *find* myself. Jesus does not demand that the *me* who is uniquely created in the image of God disintegrates or disappears. Instead Christ calls me to know how he has made me, how he has gifted me, and he calls me to bring these God-given aspects of myself to the body of believers. In contrast, when I give myself over to another I cease to have hopes, wants, dreams, or plans of my own. Instead, I complete myself by borrowing my sense of worth from the other person. Often this results in my molding myself into *your* image of me, or at least what I suspect is your image of me. Of course, your plans for me may have nothing to do with God's plans for my life!

So, what does self-denial mean in Luke 9:23-25? When we look at this verse through the lens of Western individualism, it does become synonymous with having no self at all. However, New Testament scholar Joel B. Green (1997) suggests a different interpretation of Luke:

> Discipleship entails radical self-denial, daily crossbearing and accompanying Jesus. Because of the degree to which individuals in Roman antiquity were embedded in networks of kinship, the call to denial cannot be understood along strictly individualistic terms. Rather, to deny oneself was to set aside the relationships, the extended family of origin and inner circle of friends, by which one made up one's identity. By "radical" self-denial, then, is meant *openness to constructing a wholly new identity* not based on ethnic origins (cf. 3:7-9) or relationships of mutual obligation (e.g., 6:27-38), but *in the new community* that is centered on God and resolutely faithful to Jesus' message. Taking up the cross in its Roman context would have referred literally to the victim's carrying the crossbeam of the cross from the site of sentencing to the place of crucifixion. Within Luke's narrative, however, this act has been transformed into a metaphor by the addition of the phrase "day by day," signifying that one is to live on a daily basis as though one has been sentenced to death by crucifixion. In this sense dead to the world that opposes God's purpose, disciples are free to live according to the values of the kingdom of God proclaimed in Jesus' ministry. (pp. 372-73, emphasis added)

In Jesus' day, one's self-esteem came from one's status in the community. Jesus' call to deny self is a call to set aside those things that the world says matters if you want to be somebody. Today we do not necessarily look to family association or community social status for a sense of worth. Instead, church leaders may substitute the type of committee they chair, the size of the church they serve, the location of their church, and the number of programs their church offers for a sense of self-value. Christ's call for self-denial is a call to set aside those things that pollute my sense of myself as one who bears the image of God, who is dedicated to live according to the values of God's kingdom within the context of the community of believers for the sake of the world. It is at this point that I find myself reflected in the eyes of Jesus Christ.

How does one work on being differentiated? Family therapist Edwin Friedman (1985) speculates that you don't come close to fuller levels of differentiation of self until you reach your sixties. He quickly continues that you won't reach it at all unless you start. We recommend that you begin this work as soon as possible.

You can launch your efforts to differentiate by following these steps (Gilbert, 1992; Richardson, 2005; Titelman, 2003):

1. Become an excellent observer of how your network of relationships works as an emotional system. Get outside of your own subjective experience. Watch what is actually going on. Describe people's interactions as objectively and neutrally as possible. Ask yourself who is doing what, when, where, and how. It may help to imagine that you are an anthropologist who is studying your network of church or family relationships.

2. Become an excellent observer of *yourself*. Become curious about your own feeling states, especially about your levels of anxiety. When do you get anxious? How do you experience anxiety in your body? What do you do when you get anxious? Are you more afraid of engulfment or abandonment?

3. Develop greater objectivity about yourself and others. Here is where that anthropologist attitude will really pay off. It will help you to not take yourself so seriously! As you gain mastery over your anxiety, you will find that you can achieve a certain level of objective detachment that allows you to avoid knee-jerk reactions when people push your buttons. Grow in your awareness of how you react and respond to others. Objectivity is not the same as anxiety-driven distancing.

If you *choose* your response to others, you are not being driven by anxiety. Objectivity is also not passionlessness. Differentiated leaders can be quite passionate people, but they do not let their passion cloud their objectivity, especially at times when anxiety is escalating.

4. Lower your own reactivity and calm your anxious feelings as soon as possible. Engage your thinking to quiet your frightened emotional brain system. Breathe slowly from your diaphragm. If time permits, engage in healthy activities that you find relaxing, such as walking and gardening. You can even clean! Again, calming yourself does not mean killing your enthusiasm. You calm your fretful, fearful, anxious emotions, not your eager, thrilled, or energized ones.

5. Take a moment to think and reflect. Name the negative feelings that have been triggered. Mentally go back in time and identify what was going on at the time these negative feelings were triggered. Has this happened before, that is, is this a set pattern? Sometimes our patterns go back to our families of origin, so don't confine your thinking to your adulthood. What is this pattern about (i.e., engulfment or abandonment)? You may have to get below a layer of anger in order to detect the more vulnerable feelings of fear and sadness. Is your response appropriate for a church leader in this particular context? If you are just starting to work on differentiation, it may help to pose this kind of question to a spiritual mentor, professional counselor, or mature friend. If you have always responded in this way, then you also probably assume that your response is appropriate, even if it brings disastrous results with it. If change is desired, what options exist? Again, you may find that a spiritual mentor, professional counselor, or mature friend may help you see options that are presently outside of your awareness.

6. Let go of your unrealistic or idealistic expectations of others and of yourself. This is perhaps one of the hardest steps. When we have expectations for others, our focus is on them (*you change*), not on ourselves (*I'm anxious*). Instead of muttering about how "they" should be different, consider how *you* can respond differently when they do what they always do. Remember that differentiation is not about changing others. It is about changing you. And the change that you may need is to be less judgmental of yourself!

7. Review, rehearse, and repeat. Practice any new options that you create for yourself.

8. Find someone who can walk with you on this journey. You may find it beneficial to secure the help of a close friend, spiritual mentor, professional counselor, or mature friend to act as a kind of relationship coach during these processes. Honest comments from others may help bring tremendous insights into how you actually live.

# Self-Soothing and a Nonanxious Presence

Self-control is listed among the fruit of the Spirit (Gal 5:22). When one is highly anxious, rational, logical thought, which typically directs self-control, is quickly overtaken by neurologically driven fight-or-flight reactions (Goleman, 2006). We feel anything but in control of ourselves at these moments. Yet regaining this cognitive upper hand is essential for a well-differentiated self. Church leaders who are able to calm their anxiety are able to think more objectively and creatively. They are less susceptible to catching the anxiety of others, and are actually more likely to exert a calming influence over others. In a surprising psychological sense, calmness can be as contagious as anxiety, especially if the calmer person is one who has influence over others.

Previously we noted that Edwin Friedman's (1985) definition of differentiation of self includes the phrase: "the capacity to maintain a (relatively) nonanxious presence in the midst of anxious systems" (p. 27). What is involved in maintaining a nonanxious presence, to use Friedman's term? Essentially this is the ability to comfort yourself (Schnarch, 2002). It is the power to temper your anxiety when you sense that it is beginning to rise and to resist becoming anxious when others around you are anxious. For those in Christ, this is the decision to seek help, strength, and courage from the always present Advocate (John 14:16), who helps and counsels us in all matters. A nonanxious church leader is one who can be in the midst of an apprehensive group, continue to stay connected to them, yet calmly maintain his sense of direction in complete dependence upon the Lord. Self-soothing involves

turning inward and accessing your own resources to regain your emotional balance and feeling comfortable in your body. Your breathing is unlabored, your heart slows to its normal rate; your shoulders are relaxed, no longer hunched to ward off an anticipated blow. Self-soothing is your ability to comfort yourself, lick your own wounds, and care for yourself without excessive indulgence or deprivation. (Schnarch, 1997, p. 170)

How does self-soothing relate to spiritual maturity? According to Shults and Sandage (2006):

> In theological terms, this "self-soothing" is not a . . . reliance on one's own power to soothe but a reception of, and participation in, divine grace, by which one is consoled and learns to console others (cf. 2 Cor. 1:3-7). We understand self-soothing, as a relational construct, to mean ways of relating to self that include taking responsibility for effectively soothing anxiety. A capacity for self-soothing reduces the risk for unhealthy dependence upon others. (p. 35)

The Holy Spirit can nudge us to activate self-soothing skills and we can learn to rely upon the Holy Spirit to help us calm down. Those who are growing in spiritual maturity will remain sensitive to this urging of the Spirit instead of being caught up in the anxiety of the moment. The capacity to self-sooth is consistent with Paul's admonition to the Colossians to "rid yourselves of all such things as these: anger, rage, malice, slander, and filthy language from your lips" and "as God's chosen people, holy and dearly loved, [to] clothe yourselves with compassion, kindness, humility, gentleness and patience" (Col 3:8, 12 NIV).

Confidence in one's ability to self-soothe increases one's sense of security and safety. When you are able to keep yourself emotionally safe, you are able to stay emotionally connected with others in ways that help them feel calmer too. Science writer Daniel Goleman (2006) notes that this ability to "deescalate emotional storms" (p. 183) is an important life skill that enables us to return to a state of calm contentment of our own accord, regardless of the circumstances. Perhaps you can picture self-soothing as one aspect of experiencing the kind of peace that the Lord promised to us in John 14:25-27. Of course, God's peace surpasses any self-help technique that we might recommend. Yet we also suspect that our inability to manage our anxiety blunts our receptivity to that wonderful peace. When church leaders can self-soothe, they bring a greater sense of calm just by being present and accounted for.

How does one increase one's capacity for self-soothing? First, learn to recognize when you are beginning to get anxious. This includes knowing the signs of anxiety that first show up in your body, such as tightness in your throat, a dry mouth, sweaty palms, and an increased heart rate.

Second, as your anxiety begins to rise, activate your neurological brakes, that is, take deep, calming breaths, lower the volume of your voice, slow the rate of your speech, unclench your teeth or your fists. Third, as with differentiation, adopt an objective and neutral attitude about the situation. You do not assume that you understand other people's motives, thoughts, or feelings. Nor do you assume that you know what is best for another. Instead, you become curious about how they came to the conclusions that they drew. Fourth, if your anxiety continues to rise and you think "I probably shouldn't say this . . . ," then take your own advice and remain quiet. You have just signaled yourself that you need a moment longer to calm down so that you can think more clearly. Fifth, monitor what you say to yourself. Are you talking to yourself in ways that will settle you down, such as: "I can manage this"; "I am not in danger"; "I have options at this moment"? Or are you thinking in ways that are guaranteed to increase your anxiety: "I can't believe you're saying this to me! I can't stand this! This is awful. I can't believe this is happening! You can't treat me like this! Who do you think you are!?" We suggest the former line of thoughts is more consistent with self-soothing than the latter.

While it would be lovely if others would change in ways that made our lives less anxious, it isn't necessary! Self-soothing does not take two. Family therapist David Schnarch (1997) writes:

> Self-soothing involves meeting two core challenges of selfhood: (a) not losing yourself to the pressures and demands of others, and (b) developing your capacity for self-centering (stabilizing your own emotions and fears). Sometimes we miss the chance to become self-*centering* and self-soothing because we fear becoming self-*centered*—selfish, self-preoccupied, and indifferent to others. . . . Our ability to maintain ourselves in close emotional proximity to [others] doesn't lead to self-interest at their expense. Differentiation helps us tolerate the tension in recognizing our partners as separate individuals with competing preferences, needs, and agendas. (p. 173)

Remember that self-soothing is not inconsistent with our humble dependence on the Holy Spirit. Christ sent the Comforter to us for just that purpose. Nevertheless, many of us may find that instead of looking to the Holy Spirit to help us calm ourselves, we look to others to change in order for us to be perfectly calm. The capacity to self-soothe will help us lean into the love of the Trinity more fully because we will no longer be looking to other frail human beings for our sense of significance and security.

# Self-Responsibility

A final aspect of differentiation of self is the call to a life of integrity. Integrity can be defined as moral soundness, or *the ability to live by* one's moral code of ethics. David Schnarch (1997) describes personal integrity as

> living according to your own values and beliefs in the face of opposition. It is also the ability to change your values, beliefs, and behavior when your well-considered judgment or concern for others dictates it. Putting [others'] goals on a par with your own and delaying your agenda accordingly takes (and makes) integrity. (pp. 47-48)

Self-responsibility seen through the lens of integrity includes answering the following questions: Am I living according to Christ's call on my life? Am I being the kind of person that Christ calls me to be in *this* situation? Am I living according to my Christian beliefs, values, and intentions? This includes doctrinal truth. But in a larger sense, it includes what we hold to be true about the kind of person we believe that God has created us to be. Scripture may not specify the city in which you should live, but it does specify the characteristics and attitudes of those who are church leaders (i.e., Col 3:1-17). Self-responsibility challenges church leaders to act with the utmost integrity and to respond to difficult situations in ways that honor Christ and edify the body of believers. Paul's challenge to the Colossians is a call to self-responsibility. For example, Paul writes: "Bear with each other and forgive one another if any of you has a grievance against someone. Forgive as the Lord forgave you. And over all these virtues put on love, which binds them all together in perfect unity" (Col 3:13-14 TNIV).

Acting with integrity is easy when your anxiety is low. It becomes most challenging when relationship anxiety is present. While you may wish that you did not have to experience these personally defining moments, it is *exactly* at these times of choice that you actually strenghten your "internal integrity muscles." How does this happen? First, when you realize that your anxiety is rising, stop and pray. Seek the calming presence of the Holy Spirit. Second, ask the Spirit to show you the wisest course of action. This will not necessarily be the *easiest* path. Third, practice being a non-anxious presence when you feel provoked. Notice that these actions do not set up the church leader as imperial dictator because they include aspects of humility. They do, however, charge the church leader to be accountable for himself and his display of emotions.

Self-responsibility also includes taking ownership of how you have contributed to any relationship mess in which you may find yourself. According to Scripture, God created humanity as choice-making beings who are *subsequently responsible for their own behavior.* When you take ownership for how you have contributed to the relationship tension in which you find yourself, you are living out of this creation reality. Yet like Adam and Eve we are more aware of how others have acted on us or against us than we are aware of how we have acted toward them. Like Adam and Eve, we are more comfortable blaming others than owning up. Consider the times that you may have thought or even said, "If you hadn't _____, then I wouldn't have _____." The point of self-responsibility is that others may influence what you choose to do in a relationship, but they do not *cause* you to react in that way. Ronald Richardson (2005) says it succinctly, "We don't make people behave badly toward us, but we do play a part. Do we know what it is we do?" (p. 136).

To address this aspect of self-responsibility, you may want to answer the following questions as they relate to a specific leadership dilemma that you may experience:

♦ How do I contribute to the tension in the group? Am I aware of how much relationship anxiety affects my actions and words?
♦ What do others see when I become filled with anxiety?
♦ How might they then interpret my words and reactions?
♦ What do others do when I show my anxiety?
♦ How do I subsequently react to them?
♦ Can I look at myself through the eyes of other people without defending myself or blaming them?
♦ When they tell me how they experience me, do I consider what they say or immediately reject it?

Family therapist Philip Guerin and associates (1996) propose that self-responsibility allows us "to work at seeing the parts of ourselves that contribute significantly to our own pain and our relationship discomfort. . . . [It] is the ability to see a relationship problem as a result not only of the other person's limitation but also of one's own" (p. 43). In the vignette at the beginning of this chapter, we find that twice Royce wanted to avoid this component of differentiation of self. If you recall, he denied his grow-ing intimacy with Mary when his wife confronted him about her worries. Then he wanted to avoid the consequences of his betrayal by moving to a new church in another location, rather than admitting what he had done.

Self-responsibility challenges us to take the log out of our own eye before poking our fingers in our neighbor's eye to remove the speck found there (Matt 7:3-5). Self-responsibility calls us to tend to our side of the relationship problem instead of telling others how they need to change to make us more comfortable. As long as you are blaming the other person for the relationship crisis in which you find yourself, you will remain a victim and will most likely be a less effective church leader. However, when you turn your attention to how *you* contributed to the relationship pain, then you can and should do something about that. You will no longer be a victim. Instead you will be a person of integrity.

Self-responsibility does not affirm that individuals contributed equally to relationship problems. Nor does it deny that in some cases a "pure vic-tim" does exist. However, by the time we reach adulthood, it is highly unlikely that we are *totally* innocent. That designation tends to be reserved for the truly powerless, such as children, who have no options when they are wounded by the hands of more powerful adults. Self-responsibility also does not mean that you take responsibility for every-thing wrong about the relationship. You take responsibility for your portion of the problems—*no more and no less*. If you remove the burden of responsibility from others' shoulders, then you are in effect denying them the opportunity to grow and mature. The Apostle Paul identified this tendency in some of us when he wrote in Romans 12:18 "If it is pos-sible, *as far as it depends on you*, live at peace with everyone" (NIV, emphasis added). Too often our tendency is to deny responsibility for our-selves while we focus exclusively on how others need to be responsible. Paul's admonition encourages us to do just the opposite. It is a call to be responsible *for ourselves* and to live responsibly *toward others*. In this way you live as a person of integrity.

# Going On to Maturity

Newton's Third Law says that for every action there is an equal (in size) and opposite (in direction) reaction force. If you decide to become a more clearly defined self, not everyone will rise up and call you blessed! Differentiation of self has consequences for others who are in relationship with you. As a church leader, you are already embedded in different relationship webs that count on you to act in certain ways. When you change, you challenge others to change also, and they may not be particularly happy with that challenge. For example, if you are the over-responsible church leader, becoming a self may mean that you stop doing everything for everyone. You may risk saying no to someone who expects you to say yes. If you tend to cave in through under responsibility, it means that you will actually follow through when you make a promise to complete a task, and you will do this with minimal or no grumbling and complaining. The people who have picked up your slack won't know what to make of this change and come to your rescue because that is what they have always done. If you tend to withdraw, it means that you will show up and be emotionally present during important discussions. When others experience these changes in you, their first reaction is not necessarily going to be "Thank you for challenging me to finish growing up too!" You need to be prepared for sabotage, for others to react to you in ways that invite you to change back to your old, less-differentiated self. Your act of differentiation will actually increase anxiety in others, even if it decreases your own experience of anxiety in the long run. It is imperative at this point that you remain clear on where you are heading and not let yourself get caught up in others' reactivity.

Is all of this worth the effort? We believe that it is because we believe that this is congruent with our call to "go on to maturity" (Heb 6:1 NIV).

CHAPTER FIVE

# RELATIONAL HOLINESS:
# INTERPERSONAL MATURITY

*Some from Chloe's household have informed me that there are quarrels among you.—1 Cor 1:11 NIV*

When I (Toddy) was in high school, I had to take geometry. While I was quite capable of identifying basic shapes like circles, squares, rectangles, and triangles, I was less capable of mastering the mathematics that were associated with these shapes. The formulas were mysterious and the calculations were difficult. During one particularly frustrating homework session, my mother suggested that I use my imagination to picture the shapes as I worked through the problems. Although my experience was not as dramatic as Saint Paul's conversion, suddenly the scales fell off my eyes and I could see! I did not become a geometry genius, but I was now able to pass the class because I saw things differently.

A certain kind of geometry also affects our relationships. Relationship geometry comes into play when you feel like a third wheel or when you think two's company, but three's a crowd. You are also caught up in relationship geometry if someone tells you something negative about another person with the intent to change your relationship with that absent party. Few soap operas would last for more than a month if it weren't for relationship geometry of this kind! More to our point, a certain kind of relationship geometry tends also to affect church leadership. For example, relationship geometry is at work if in the midst of a heated debate a committee colleague wants you to take up his side of the argument against the person with whom he disagrees. Perhaps more common is when the pastor is called in to negotiate a truce between two or more feuding family members, let alone two or more feuding families! Family therapists (Friedman, 1985; Guerin, et al., 1996; Richardson, 1996) have identified the *triangle* as one geometric shape that plays into many leadership problems. Relationship triangles develop when two people are unable to contain the anxiety (and subsequent brewing conflict) that has built up between them—like two angry church members. To reduce this anxiety, they turn to a third party—like the pastor. This is called *triangulation*.

Family therapist Philip Guerin (1996) says, "Remember, without becoming paranoid, that every individual or couple you deal with is a problem in search of a triangle" (p. 12). While Guerin was referring to people seeking therapy, we believe that he also could have been talking about the local church. It seems that many of our churches use triangulation as their standard operating procedure. Not surprisingly these are also the churches where congregational leaders have difficulty sharing power, where pastors may act like dictators instead of shepherds, and where churches are known to chew up and spit out one pastor after another. We suggest that immature leaders excel at generating and maintaining emotional triangles while mature church leaders know how to remain available to others in need without getting sucked into a destructive triangle. In this chapter we will explore how lower levels of differentiation plus higher levels of anxiety promote the creation of leadership triangles. We will also discuss how leaders can cope with triangles by maintaining a nonanxious presence. We hope that you will see how the aspects of relational holiness that we explored in previous chapters—anxiety, spiritual and emotional maturity—come into play in situations involving triangles. The following vignette provides an example for our conversation about emotional triangles.

Ben slowly opened the folder that lay before him. He had postponed creating the agenda for the next local board of administration meeting far too long, and now he really needed to review the business that they had conducted last month in preparation for this upcoming meeting. As he thumbed through the folder's contents, his thoughts drifted back to the last meeting. The agenda had seemed straightforward enough at the time. Reports were given and received. Old business was managed without a hitch. Then they came to new business. Pastor Tom had added an item, "approval of new chairs," to the agenda at the beginning of the meeting. Ben had assumed that "approval of new chairs" meant that the nomination committee had successfully recruited leaders for the next year, and that Pastor Tom was presenting the slate of candidates to the local board of administration. Ben did not realize that the pastor was actually proposing to remove the traditional oak pews in the sanctuary, and to replace them with moveable, padded, folding chairs.

Pastor Tom presented his proposal to the board. He noted that the chairs were to be a gift from a neighboring church that was moving into a new facility. Pastor Tom suggested that this unexpected gift would provide a greater degree of flexibility and comfort during worship, and would allow the worship center to serve multiple purposes. Logically, this proposal was consistent with the board's desire to bring their church out of the 1950s and into the twenty-first century. It was already apparent that changes in the worship service held greater appeal for the younger families who lived near the church than had their traditional worship service. Pastor Tom commented that this would be just one more step in the right direction.

The general discussion had started out calm and cordial. But then Ben sat there in shock as the meeting somehow turned ugly. Several members of the board strongly objected to the very idea of removing the pews. "If these pews go, then I go!" said one of the board's senior saints. The pillars of the church murmured their assent. Others, primarily the younger and newer members of the board, strongly objected to *not* removing the pews. "You don't pass up an opportunity to receive 300 free, padded folding chairs!" one woman said. As the tension in the room increased, Ben watched Pastor Tom emotionally shut down and tune out. Ben suspected that the pastor was taking this debate as a personal attack rather than seeing the intensity of board members' responses as an indication that some older members were emotionally invested in the old oak pews. What made Ben really uncomfortable was when each speaker looked at Ben as if to secure Ben's allegiance and vote. Ben felt caught in the middle. He wanted to continue the progress that Pastor Tom had begun, but he personally liked the beauty of the oak pews and the history that they represented. Most of all, he was surprised at the intensity of his own emotional resistance to their removal. He needed more time to sort this out. Ben finally got the board to agree to pray about the matter and to table the motion until the next meeting.

The intervening month was difficult for Ben. Each week Ben received phone calls and emails from different board members who wanted to recruit Ben to their side and who tried to persuade Ben to apply pressure to the pastor to either stay the course or give it up. In addition, Ben had gotten a call from Pastor Tom, who asked Ben to forward to him all emails that board members sent to Ben about the issue and to report to Pastor Tom any phone conversations that Ben had about the topic with other board members so that the pastor would have the inside scoop and would know how to play his cards at the next meeting. Ben suspected that board members were beginning to talk negatively about one another and the pastor to different people in the congregation. What was he going to do?

# How Are Relationship Triangles Created?

Triangles form any time two people pull in a third person or thing to help them manage their reactivity. There is good news and bad news about triangles. The good news: triangles are a normal part of human relationships. Even the most astute among us will get triangled at one time or another. The bad news: triangulation is habit-forming because triangles work. They *do* lower anxious reactivity, but only temporarily. In addition, they rob individuals of an opportunity to mature spiritually, emotionally, and relationally.

Ben was caught in the middle of a powerful emotional triangle. The members of this triangle were Pastor Tom, the administrative board, and Ben. As the anger mounted in the meeting, so did the anxiety within individual board members and between the board members. Ben, having been caught off guard by the rapidly rising anxiety, was unable to remain calm and objective in the moment. That is, he was unable to maintain a nonanxious presence. Pastor Tom was also overcome by the anxiety in the meeting. At this point you may have recalled our previous discussion in chapter 2 about gridlock and the two-choice dilemma. Gridlock happens when groups get stuck and are unable to move forward without incurring uncomfortable levels of anxiety. People are then caught in the two-choice dilemma—they want to do as they please and they want to dictate how others will respond to them. In this case Pastor Tom wanted to present his motion and have the board approve it without any hassles. This is not an unrealistic expectation for many administrative council motions. Gridlock blossomed when Pastor Tom did not get his way. We mentioned three typical, but unhelpful, ways to deal with gridlock: to withdraw (Pastor Tom), to take over (some board members), or to give over (perhaps Ben).[1] Gridlocked situations are fertile soil for triangles because both involve an inability to manage one's anxiety.

Another way to picture the process of triangulation is to return to our crucible metaphor, also from chapter 2. Think about emotional anxiety as what is swirling around inside the crucible along with a distressed dynamic duo. When the relationship is not strong enough to contain the anxious reactivity, a buildup of pressure fractures the crucible. At this point everything inside the crucible spills out. If the duo regroups (self-responsibility), calms down (self-soothing), and stays connected (differentiation of self), then they can resume dealing with their concerns in a relatively nonanxious and more objective manner. Triangulation happens when *someone else* comes along or is invited to help clean up the relationship muddle. In other words, the conditions for a triangle are *primed* when two people struggle to calm the anxiety that lies within them and between them. A triangle is *activated* only when a third person (i.e., an affair) or thing (i.e., an addiction) gets involved.

Think back to the local board of administration meeting. You can picture the tension mounting between Pastor Tom and his "opposition." At this point the triangle pump is only primed. Ben's position as chair of the board sets him up as one of the most likely persons to be triangled between these two opponents. If he assumes emotional responsibility for making all members of the board happy, he has just activated the triangle by his actions. Let us be clear. It *is* Ben's responsibility to conduct the meeting and manage the discussions. Here is where *Robert's Rules of Order* can actually be helpful, as it provides a structure for intense discussions of this nature. Ben is invited into a triangle when board members look to him to support their side. Whether or not a Ben/board/Pastor Tom triangle will be activated will depend on Ben.

Church leadership is an area riddled with triangle quicksand. By definition, leadership is a type of helping relationship, which means that church leaders in general and pastors in particular either host or get invited into triangles *as a normal part of life*. Often the invitation to participate in a triangle is subtle, and the opportunity to ride to somebody's rescue and bail people out of messes is too hard for many church leaders to resist. Unfortunately, triangles tend to be persistent, pervasive, and permanent. Like weeds in one's spiritual and emotional garden, they will soon choke the life out of good intentions. In the end they restrain growth in relational holiness.

I (Steve) well remember the temptations to enter relational triangles that I faced during the pressing times of building campaigns. Despite the obvious need for increased space, a careful, well-thought-out rationale for the addition, and a thorough process to solicit input from all of the stakeholders regarding the new plan, there were always some who were against the whole thing. The easy and almost automatic default road at the time was to work with my key leaders who were obviously for the project while neglecting the insights, opinions, and the very real emotions of those who were against it. While not denying that there will be times when, for the sake of the overall good of the body, church leaders must press ahead with decisions that will be unpopular with some, we must also say that to pit members who agree with us against those who don't (triangulation) can be devastating to the well-being of individuals and the body as a whole. As a church leader you may win a battle for a project, but through relational triangles you can quite possibly end up losing the war for your overall effectiveness as a pastoral presence.

If church leaders and pastors aren't emotionally and relationally intelligent (Goleman, 1995, 2006), they will quickly sink in triangle quicksand. You know you are being triangled when you carry the burden for the relationship between the other two. You have reached this point when it seems as if you are spending more time and energy on the problem than the original two people are investing in working on their relationship. Or you may have been triangled if you find yourself acting as the judge who is settling a dispute between a plaintiff and a defendant. Certainly, you are being triangled if you are working an "us against them" campaign. Does this mean that church leaders should never offer an opinion? No, it doesn't. If the church leader shares his or her opinion calmly or even enthusiastically without getting agitated if the other two reject it, then that leader is not being triangled during that exchange. Does it mean that a pastoral counselor should not answer a question that has been raised in a counseling session? Not necessarily. It really depends on the question! Questions of fact should most likely be answered.

Questions of opinion get a bit stickier. At this juncture the pastoral counselor may want to ask: Is it really necessary for me to give my opinion on this matter? What is the motivation behind the question?[2] Later in this chapter we will explore how to stay connected to others with Christlike compassion and to offer help without volunteering for the open spot in an emotional triangle.

How do third parties form a triangle? Two common ways are through recruiting or volunteering. A classic example of recruitment happens when a parent uses a child as a confidant instead of talking with the other parent face-to-face. As the child grows, she unconsciously assumes responsibility for her parents' marriage. For some young adults, this means that they are unable to leave home emotionally. They may also struggle to "leave and cleave" when they marry. I (Toddy) once counseled a couple in which the wife delighted to watch her thirteen-year-old daughter "take on" her father. This wife was emotionally estranged from her husband and was not able to tell him what she wanted from him. When the daughter talked back to her father, the mother silently cheered her on. Eventually this daughter went to college in another state to get away from her family. However, her worry about her parent's marriage interfered with her studies. She returned home after one semester because she feared that her parents would divorce if she didn't continue to help them stay married.

Recruitment is active in our vignette. Tension exists between different factions of the board (pro-pews/pro-chairs) and Pastor Tom. As people become more reactive, various board members look at Ben, the chair, to take their side. Through their glance, Ben is being recruited to be the third person in a triangle comprised of the speaker, Pastor Tom, and Ben. If Ben fails to self-soothe and instead *anxiously reacts* when the other person catches his eye, then he is on the brink of being triangled. However, if he remains calm, thoughtful, objective, and neutral, and if others take that as a cue to calm down also, then Ben may avoid being triangled. Unfortunately, however, the recruitment drive continues during the weeks following the council meeting. Council members ask Ben to talk to Pastor Tom *and* Pastor Tom asks Ben to give him the "inside scoop." As you can see, Ben is now in a triangle hot seat and Pastor Tom is perilously close to dividing members of the congregation against one another.

If someone isn't actively recruited into a triangle, he may volunteer to be the third party. A typical example from the home would be the child who tells her parents to stop fighting on a regular basis. One of my (Toddy) former clients exhausted herself caring for others in her church. She particularly got caught up in mediating others' problems. What made her a triangle junkie instead of a peacemaker was that, rather than an authentic call of God, it was her own emotional reactivity that *drove* her to do these things. She became involved where she had not been invited. She became highly distressed when others rejected her suggestions. Later in this chapter we will show you how Pastor Tom's wife, Patricia, volunteered for triangle duty. If one of your life mottoes happens to be, "I never heard of a problem that I didn't feel obligated to fix," then we suspect that you may be a seasoned triangle volunteer as well.

## Threesomes and Triangles

At this point you may be wondering if *all* three-person relationships are triangles. *They aren't.* Three people can strongly disagree or they can be very close and not become a triangle. Family therapist Philip Guerin and colleagues (1996) differentiate between healthy three-person relationships (triads, trios, threesomes) and triangles. Guerin describes a wholesome triad as follows:

> A threesome can be broken down into three simultaneous twosomes— that is, three interconnected twosomes that simultaneously are in some kind of distant (relatively uninvolved) or a close, intensely involved relationship. All three members can interact with each other, one-on-one, depending on what the situation calls for. They have options. They can choose to be involved or uninvolved and to vary their involvement so that it isn't necessarily reactive and predictable (such as always being angry or always being sympathetic). Each member of the threesome can take an honest, diplomatic "I" position with any other member of the threesome without trying to change the other two or trying to impose that position on the others. Each member can allow the other two to have their own relationship, work out their own problems, and enjoy their particular pleasures, without interfering to "make peace," to instigate conflict, or to side with one against the other. It is characteristic of a threesome that each person in a threesome has a sense of freedom and an ability to focus on self rather than looking to see where the others stand before taking his or her own stand—in other words, being determined by them. (p. 46)

In many ways, the Trinity functions as an ideal threesome. Again, it does help that the members of the Godhead share perfect, self-giving love. Nevertheless, if you look at Guerin's description of a healthy triad, you can see how the members of the Triune God metaphorically interrelate in such a manner. Of course, one cannnot imagine any kind of relationship anxiety permeating the relationship of the Trinity! And this is where the comparison breaks down. The challenge to remain a triad rather than becoming a triangle only exists when relationship anxiety is lurking around the corner. So what would a healthy threesome look like? First, each twosome could relate independent of the third person. For example, two of the three could go out to lunch, and the third person wouldn't get angry. Second, each person could make his or her own decisions about how to act when tension mounted between them, and each one could speak his or her mind (taking an "I" position) on matters under discussion without trying to change the minds of the others. If one twosome has a falling out, the third party may be concerned, but this third party also feels no obligation to jump in and fix this distressed relationship. She trusts that they can work it out themselves. Finally, each one takes responsibility for the impact of his words and actions. There is no cop-out of "you made me do this or that."

Triangles would have the opposite characteristics. As we said before, triangles are a part of life. People create and dissolve triangles based on situational or developmental stresses that they face. When relationship anxiety is absent, an existing triangle is dormant. When anxiety floods the relationship, the triangle is activated. While triangles tend to be permanent and persistent (fixed), they can also be temporary and time limited (fluid). If individuals can respond to stress with creative options, they transform their fixed triangle into a fluid one, and even minimize triangulation altogether. However, when people are stuck in a rut of knee-jerk actions and reactions, they are most likely also stuck in a fixed triangle. It is *this* kind of triangle in which one needs to exercise spiritual and emotional maturity most fully.

# Why Do Triangles Work?

Family therapist Edwin Friedman (1985, pp. 36-39) proposed seven interrelated principles that are at work whenever triangles are activated. These principles explain *why* triangles work. To help you see these principles at work, we continue our vignette. We discuss the seven principles following the vignette.

Pastor Tom is upset that his proposal to replace the oak pews with padded folding chairs has been tabled. Patricia, his wife, knows that something is wrong as soon as he walks in the door. She talks with Tom about the meeting late into the night, reaffirming the rightness of Tom's proposal. She actually thinks that Tom sprang his proposal on the board too quickly. However, she fears that Tom will emotionally withdraw from her if he thinks that she is criticizing him in any way. She tells Tom that she will do what she can to help spread the word about Tom's wonderful idea as a way to calm Tom and to reassure herself. Tom has a pleasant night and Patricia sleeps fitfully. In the ensuing weeks, Patricia calls the wives of other influential church members and paints a picture of an obstinate, backward-looking board with a wimpy chairperson. She encourages the wives to talk with their husbands and to have their husbands apply pressure to the opposition council members.

Some readers at this point may be thinking, "Well, that's just the way that church politics work." This may indeed be true—that many church groups operate this way and that decisions become pawns in a triangle. But this "business as usual" process comes with a *huge* price. Triangles keep less-secure people from offering creative solutions in order to avoid becoming somebody's next target. Gossip and rumors are nurtured through triangulation. Conflicts are fanned into raging fires. Finally, triangles erode trust and tend to push people into more extreme positions. In other words, everyone blames the other for the problem, the situation continues to escalate, and there seems to be no solution in sight.

**Principle 1: The relationship of any two members of an emotional triangle is kept in balance by the way a third party relates to each of them or to their relationship.**

We expect that Patricia will care about the outcome of the board meeting. This is normal. If she is able to care about Tom *without absorbing Tom's anxiety*, then she can respond with empathy to his dilemma without rushing in anxiously to fix the situation for him. Or she may also take an "I" position ("I think you presented the proposal prematurely" or "I wonder what would help you understand the intense reaction of the other members?"). If she can stay connected to Tom and say this calmly and objectively, Tom may pick up on her calmness. However, this is not what happened. Patricia becomes the third person who helps to balance the relationship between Tom and the local board of administration.

If Tom wanted to avoid inviting Patricia into a triangle and take personal responsibility for his leadership, he could take time to ask himself the following questions: At what point in the discussion did I begin to lose my cool? What was I thinking when that happened? How do I think the board experienced me at this point? How did different board members respond to my proposal? What was happening when things began to spin out of control? Who got upset first? Who else got caught up in this? How did that process unfold? What did I do then? What other options were available to me at that point? What other issues might have been behind the scenes that might have primed everyone's reactivity to my proposal? What can I do to stay calmer in future discussions? What relationships might I need to repair at this point? These questions will help Tom reflect about the meeting and gain self-control instead of remaining reactive and divisive.

**Principle 2: The change that the third party brings to an emotional triangle will last for a few weeks. The effects of trying to change the relationship between two other people directly are temporary.**

This principle indicates why we continue to participate as the third party in emotional triangles—our efforts to bring change to the relationship between two other people works *temporarily*! When the effects wear off, then we have to renew our efforts yet again. If you have been trying to convince two of your children *to want to* change how they act toward each other, we suspect that you have also said, "How many times do I have to remind you . . . ?" Because you hold the power card in your family, you can dictate behavioral change. But according to this principle, the change will be short-lived. You might control their behavior, but you cannot will them into a change of attitude. It is a startling realization to many church leaders to discover that they cannot will their congregations into change. Only the Holy Spirit can do this.

Are we suggesting that Pastor Tom's wife sit by and do nothing but listen to her husband because any involvement on her part will only bring about temporary change? In this particular case, that may indeed be her best way to express her love for Tom. If she can get a grip on her anxious need to fix the situation for Tom and *not ride to his rescue*, she can then offer him the kind of emotional connection that will help him to grow and mature, to differentiate, as a leader and to truly move into a deeper level of love for those he is called to serve. On the other hand, if Tom could see the Tom-Patricia-board triangle as it develops, he could also kindly ask her to not make the phone calls and reassure her that the Lord is going to help him manage the situation. Stepping out of a triangle does not mean that you stop caring for people or that you stop praying for those you care about and the situation. It does mean that you stop others from doing your work for you or you stop doing their work for them (and, yes, this does mean that they may not do that work for themselves. This presents a challenge for you to work on your anxious over functioning in response to their under functioning).

**Principle 3: Trying to change the relationship of the other two sides of the triangle will be met with resistance, and you might only succeed in bringing about the opposite of your intent.**

We think that the phrase "no good deed goes unpunished" summarizes principle 3 quite nicely. For example, the parents with a daughter of dating age may know that if they vigorously oppose a person that their daughter is dating, there is a greater likelihood that she will fall madly in love with him and feel that she can't live without him. Her emotional fusion with her beau will be in proportion to her parents' efforts to break them up.[3] As it relates to our vignette, the harder Tom's wife works to win people over to Tom's position, the more likely she is to find that people have become entrenched in their opposition to or support for the folding chairs. Of course, since both Tom and his wife are unaware that they have activated a triangle, they will end up blaming the other people for their stubbornness or praise them for their sensitivity to God's directing rather than seeing how they themselves may have contributed to the increased polarization in the board and subsequently in the church as a whole.

**Principle 4: As the third party's efforts to change the relationship between the other two in an emotional triangle fail, the third party will likely end up carrying the stress for the other two.**

In our vignette Patricia is trying to change the relationship between Tom and the opposing board members. Notice that what is at work here is that the third party is becoming more and more invested, even fused, in the relationship between the other two. Because the changes are *temporary*, they are inevitably doomed to fail. The more the other two revert, the more responsible the third party will feel to fix the relationship. While Pastor Tom is upset, it is his wife who loses sleep over the matter. She wants control—to make others think the way she does—so she contacts all of her friends. We predict that she will have more sleepless nights ahead.

**Principle 5: The triangles in an emotional system will interlock so that efforts to bring change in one triangle will reverberate in others. The result may be that the other triangles will exert greater resistance to the change than the third party can overcome.**

Friedman (1985) observes that one triangle may be primary in the interlocking triangle system. In our vignette, the primary triangle is between Pastor Tom, the board, and Ben. Then the anxiety spilled over into other triangles in the church (i.e., the triangle comprised of Pastor Tom, Patricia, and Patricia's friends). More triangles will be created as each of the wife's friends involves her husband. See figure 5.1 for a picture of some of the interlocking triangles in Pastor Tom's church. If you think this looks like a rocket heading straight for Ben, the board chair, then you have correctly assessed the kind of pressure that Ben may be feeling.

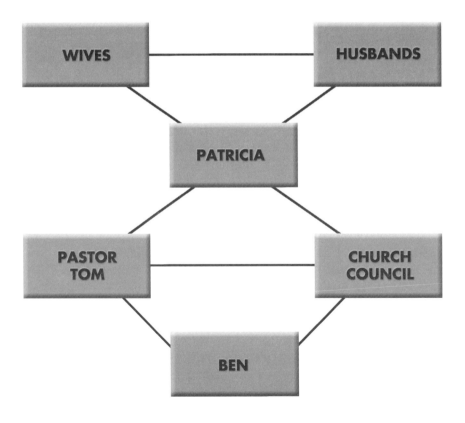

*Figure 5.1*

**Principle 6: One side of the triangle is usually more conflicted than the other two.**

In less healthy emotional systems, one side of the triangle will tend to hold most of the tension. In healthier emotional systems, the tension is shared or moves between various stakeholders in the triangle. The more fluid the tension, that is, the more that it moves around, the greater the likelihood for a creative response. For example, in family settings, one parent may be continually at odds with one particular child, with the other parent (or even other children) trying to referee their conflicts. Alternatively, I (Steve) can offer an example of shared tension.

I (Steve) recall with gratitude how in the midst of informational sessions where the congregation was asked to offer feedback regarding proposed major ministry directives to the leadership team, the leadership team and I shared the overall responsibilities for the session, including responding to the concerns of others within the congregation. When the team saw that I was getting frustrated with some of the negative criticism in public meetings, they were quick to stand up and help shoulder that criticism. The tension between me as the senior pastor and negative voices within the congregation was shared within the leadership team, and I escaped triangulation.

**Principle 7: We can only change a relationship to which we belong.**

Here is where the rubber really meets the road. The way to exert your influence when two other people invite you into a triangle is to maintain the kind of relationship with each one of them that is based on your own differentiation. You take clear "I" positions based on your values and beliefs, and avoid trying anxiously to fix their relationship. The skill is to be *non-anxious and present;* to be clear about your own beliefs *and* to be in relationship with all persons involved. In our example above, Pastor Tom could choose to lower his anxiety so that when his wife offers to call out her personal cavalry to ride to his rescue, he can respond, "Honey, I love that you care about me so much but I don't want you to do that. With the Lord's help I can and will manage my relationship with the other members of the board instead. I do need your love and prayers as I walk through this process."

# What Does Triangulation Have to Do with Relational Holiness?

At this point you may be raising several valuable questions. Perhaps you are asking: How does pastoral leadership and care relate to triangulation? What do I do about the requests I get from people in my church who are asking for my help to deal with their son or daughter or husband or wife? If I get involved, am I automatically in a triangle? What in the world does this have to do with relational holiness? To answer these questions, we have to see how differentiation of self, triangulation, and caring for others correlate.

Let's start with differentiation. You may recall that differentiation is the ability to be an "I" while remaining appropriately connected to others. In our relationship with God, differentiation helps us keep straight that we are not God; that God is God. However, we are created in the image of God and we are to conform to the image of Christ by the power of the Holy Spirit. Among other things this means that the Triune God invites us to relate intimately with God, and to reflect the self-giving love of the Godhead within our human relationships. Within God's embrace we find ourselves, and we become more of who God created us to be. We do not merge with some amorphous cosmic consciousness, and thereby lose our own unique sense of self. Our intimate connection with God empowers us to be the "I" that God created and gifted us to be when we are with others. This is the secure base that we bring to our relationships. God is also the safe haven to which we run when we need help calming ourselves when we become flooded with relationship anxiety. Therefore, from a Christian perspective, our relationship with Christ is the firm foundation from which we encounter any relationship triangle.

In our relationship with others, differentiation allows us to live out our God-given identity within the faith community and within the world. Through differentiation we avoid absorbing others to bolster our sense of who we are. We also avoid being absorbed by others without resorting to cutoff. We can maintain our boundaries while fellowshipping with those who may be challenging to love while avoiding being triangled by them. You will recall that differentiation does not depend on the actions of the other person, but on my capacity to manage myself. As we have discussed, as we rely on the Holy Spirit, differentiation includes the capacity to maintain a relatively nonanxious presence when we are among anxious groups of people, to self-soothe when we are getting anxious ourselves, and to take responsibility for the impact of our words and actions. These are crucial capacities for managing relationship triangles. These relationship capacities *free us* to relate closely with others without fear of triangulation. We do not need to demand that *they* change to keep us less anxious, nor do we feel compelled to react to *their demands that we change* to keep them less anxious. These are the very relationship skills that will help us minimize the number of times that we launch triangles.

Differentiated church leaders are thereby *freer* to choose to make sacrifices for the sake of others (Holeman, 2004). They give of themselves out of love for Christ and for others, not out of guilt and duty. Sacrificing out of a sense of duty breeds bitterness and resentment if the other, for whom we sacrifice, does not respond with gratitude or appreciation. "They never even bothered to say thanks" reflects this sentiment, and it would be indicative of a relationship triangle. While differentiated sacrifice welcomes words of thanks, it does not require it. The sacrifice was freely chosen and freely given, just like Christ's sacrifice on our behalf. No triangulation required.

Differentiation supports spiritual discernment: When do I step in and help? When is my helping actually harmful? Because differentiation includes the capacity to be less anxiously reactive, differentiated church leaders can evaluate more accurately whether or not their actions will foster dependence and immaturity in others, rather than challenging them to go on to maturity in Christ and to grow up interpersonally. From the viewpoint of differentiation, church leaders do not give in to the urge to become consistently over responsible for another in ways that would allow the other to remain under responsible.

Differentiation is not the opposite of agape love, the basis for our Christian compassion. Instead, we suggest that differentiation is a maturation process that can *enhance* our capacity to extend agape love to another human being. Agape love does not mean that we leap to everybody's rescue as soon as the phone rings! That is more indicative of a blossoming triangle. Just as God is not a heavenly bellman, we are also not bellmen for Jesus. We are called to be servant leaders following Christ's example. This means that we do not lord our leadership positions over others and bask in the glory of our power to dictate and demand. Instead it means that we seek to empower others to serve God, the community of faith, and the world for the sake of God's kingdom so that we can bring the good news of Jesus Christ to a hurting world.

Triangles will diminish our capacity to do just that. You may recall that triangles form when two people are not able or choose not to manage the anxiety that is between them. They rely on a third person to help them do this. On the one hand, you may say, "Isn't this the call of Christ for the church leader, to help others when they need help?" While the call of Christ may indeed be for us to come alongside of one another in a time of need, Scripture does not spell out in detail everything that we could do. The exact form that coming alongside takes will depend on the situation, the people involved, the overall context of the situation, past experiences, and so on. Discernment is definitely required! On the other hand, a corollary to this call of servanthood is the call for all members of the community of faith to go on to maturity, to not remain spiritual infants, to support one another in the process of growing in Christ. Triangles prevent people from maturing. When you succumb to a triangle, you rob people of the opportunity to strengthen their capacity for managing anxiety. If you always ride to the rescue, you are ensuring another's *immaturity* in a particular part of their emotional and relational life.

It is very tempting for the church leader to participate in relationship triangles. Others will look to you as their emotional savior. If church leaders have an insecure sense of who they are, this adoration by another acts as a bolster to their sense of self. The problem is that this type of church leadership requires followers to remain dependent upon the leader, or in the language of Bowenian family therapy, to remain fused with them. While the leader will say that she wants her people to grow, the leader will become anxious when an important "fused follower" begins the process of differentiation, of becoming mature. The church leader will feel the emotional pulling away. If this fused follower doesn't need the church leader anymore, the church leader is left with a hole in her "self." The leader will either find another needy follower who is ready for fusion, or will find a way to challenge her own anxiety and continue a process of growing up.

# Dealing with Triangles

What can you do, then, to deal with relationship triangles? For those of you who are action-oriented, this section may be a bit unsatisfying. Dealing with triangles is more about what you do with yourself than it is about what you do to others. It is about changing *your role* in the triangle more than it is about getting others to act differently. It is about living with the unsettled reality that when you don't play the triangle game, the other two people will find someone else who will. We can tell you that people are less likely to grow in interpersonal maturity when you participate in their triangles. The invitation to go on to maturity comes when you stay connected with them in a way that is not riddled with anxiety. In this way your level of differentiation invites them to change.

Your first task is to learn to see the triangles that currently exist in your home or your church. It is quite common for home triangles to interlock with church triangles. If your family or your church experiences gridlock, then this is an excellent place to begin looking to find triangles in action. A triangle may involve three people, two people and an issue, or three groups (such as the administrative board, the trustees, and the worship committee). To see the triangle, first identify the participants in the triangle. Then trace the movement of the people in the triangle. One way to do this is to ask the following questions: To whom, or to what, do people move when they begin to become reactive? Who moves toward or away from whom? Does anyone stand still metaphorically? Observe how people express their relationship anxiety. Do they want to fuse with another or do they prefer distance and cutoff? Do they take over, give over, or walk away? What role do you play in the triangle? Ask yourself, to whom or to what do I move when I get emotionally reactive? Do I prefer anxious fusion to those who agree with me or reactive distance from those who disagree with me? By answering the questions above, you gather information to help you reposition yourself in your relationship with others. Family therapist Ronald Richardson (2005) suggests that you consider these questions: "What would it look like for me to be neutral in all of this? . . . How will I maintain my position when the pressure to go back to my old way of functioning increases?" (p. 101).

Once you have identified a triangle, you now have two options. Both options allow you to stay connected with others who are in the triangle while they support you in lowering your anxiety. Option 1: You can work on your own internal emotional process so that you can stay as calm and as objective as possible. Option 2: You can try changing how you move in the triangle.

If you decide to work on your own emotional process, reflect on what things increase your anxiety. Devise a strategy for how you will calm yourself at these moments. For example, do you need to pay attention to your breathing? Deep breathing ("belly breathing") activates the body's natural calming system. Do you need to be mindful of what you are saying to yourself? Negative self-talk will keep your anxiety stirred up. Do you need to remember to look for the alternatives that exist and are currently just outside of your attention? Sometimes you need to get some distance from the situation before you can see the alternatives that are present.

If you decide to try to change how you move in the triangle, begin by figuring out whether you prefer to move toward or away from others in the triangle. If you become silent because you are too upset to speak, this is a form of moving away from others. If you tell people what they should be doing to fix themselves, then this is an example of moving toward others. You can make a *small* change in how you move in the triangle by standing still if you tend to fuse with another. This allows you to stay connected without resorting to anxious cutoff. If you tend to move away from others, you could also try standing still or you might think of one small way that you could move toward the others. For example, you could activate your listening skills to find out more about how the other person thinks or feels without challenging their thinking or telling them how they should feel. Be careful that you remain psychologically present! It is far too easy to be physically present but emotionally absent when anxiety rises.

Whatever option you choose, your next step is to observe how others in the triangle react to your change. You may not see a change right away. But if you persevere in your new actions, others will notice because you are no longer following the triangle script. At that point the powers that be will not readily cooperate with your efforts to change the triangle. They will push back. So it will be helpful if you can predict how others will act in attempting to get you *to return to your former way of being with them in the triangle.* For example, if you do not run to another person's rescue as you usually do, will that person be likely to accuse you of not caring? Of not doing your job as their pastor? Of not being a Christian? Or will they claim that they are not worthy of your efforts? That they are hopeless? That they are helpless? You will need the Holy Spirit to help you discern when help is truly needed and when help is really not going to be helpful at all.

The goal is to engage in the process of differentiation. Calm yourself so that you can be the nonanxious presence in the midst of an anxious system. Think clearly and objectively about the context and the content so that you can take an "I" position based on your beliefs and values. Richardson (2005) says it like this, "The key is calming our own anxiety, being less reactive, becoming truly neutral in how things play out, and staying well connected with everyone in the triangle" (p. 101).

When you take your "I" position, there may be times when you do agree more with one party than with the other. Through remaining nonanxious you can do this *and* stay connected to the other person as long as it depends on you. You cannot stop the other person from distancing from you, however. If the person does move away, your task is to listen, listen, and listen some more to what they think and feel without trying to change them and without giving up your own beliefs. When you take an "I" position, you can do so with energy. Being nonanxious does not mean that you are not passionate! It just means that you are not reacting out of your anxiety.

Let us emphasize again that the important point is that your focus is on how *you* act in the triangle. Self-responsibility means that you own up to your contributions and the role that you are playing in keeping triangles going. And that you take whatever steps you can to change yourself. Ronald Richardson (2005) recommends that you develop a "research stance" as a way to gain more objectivity and neutrality in triangle situations. You gain this objectivity by developing an eye to see the emotional process involved in groups instead of being distracted by the content of the conversation. Then you decide how you can contribute to making the environment calmer and safer for all participants, starting with yourself.

# CHAPTER SIX

# RELATIONAL HOLINESS AND RIGHTEOUS RELATIONSHIPS

*Now you are the body of Christ, and each one of you is a part of it.—*
*1 Cor 12:27 NIV*

Have you noticed that we never seem to experience God as one who anxiously jumps to our rescue, as if what has happened to us has caught God off guard? We may be riddled with anxiety and *we* may wonder when God will act on our behalf in that particular circumstance, but these are our feelings, not God's feelings. We may project these sentiments onto God, but the biblical narrative does not picture our God as one whose actions are driven by anxious reactivity. Nevertheless, God is not insensitive to our anxious hearts. We are told to "cast all your anxiety on him because he cares for you" (1 Pet 5:7 TNIV).

While we may always be children before our heavenly Father, God never treats us as younger than our years. What we mean by this is that God's activity within our lives and on our behalf is always in service of God's call to grow up in every way in Christ. When God cares for us, his intervention in our lives deepens spiritual maturity, develops greater capacities of emotional maturity, and promotes interpersonal maturity.

Through the power of the Holy Spirit we are enabled to embody relational holiness in ways that we may have never imagined possible. God's desire for us is wholeness, completeness, and maturity, not fragmentation, incompleteness, and immaturity. God desires for his people to live in relational righteousness.

A relational view of the Trinity (Grenz, 2001) has affected my (Toddy) understanding of Scripture in ways that have expanded my understanding of righteousness. I once pictured righteousness in terms of what I did or did not do—the "do and don't" view of holiness—so, righteous people do these things but not those things. Righteousness was also a character trait of God that I believed the Holy Spirit would develop in my life through the process of sanctification. I still believe that there are certain actions that are righteous while others are not righteous. I affirm that I am to be holy as God is holy (1 Pet 1:15, 16).

However, I now think of *righteousness* in terms of rightly relating to God and to others. For me, righteousness is now a *relational* word that describes characteristics of my relationships with others. So now I ask the following question: *What would it look like for me as a church leader to rightly relate to this person under these circumstances at this moment in time?* Of course, I am not left entirely to my own experience and opinion about righteous relationships. The biblical narrative is clear about the qualities that should characterize the relationships between God's people, even if it isn't always as clear about *how* we are to embody, enact, or live out those relationship qualities. For example, I believe that God relates to me in ways that call me to mature and grow in holiness. What helps me go on to maturity may be different than what helps you go on to maturity. Likewise, as a church leader, I too should relate to others in the *many different ways* that can call them to mature and grow in holiness. Conversely, I should avoid relating to others in ways that will foster immaturity—spiritually, emotionally, or interpersonally.

This brings us to a discussion of how church leaders express their connection to others within the church. How may church leaders' expressions of connectedness embody righteousness? When you put the question like this, you can see that righteous connections are more complex than compiling a list of dos and don'ts. In this final chapter we want to envision what some of these new patterns of relating might look like.

# Connectedness and Attachment

Earlier in this book we suggested that differentiation of self is an avenue to better relationships with others. Fred Gingrich (2004) astutely observes, and we concur, "There is a fine line between differentiating and disconnecting. In promoting self-responsibility and [individuality] as the goals of healthy relationships, the legitimate needs for deep emotional connection can sometimes be lost" (p. 33). This can easily happen when Bowen's idea of stuck-togetherness is misunderstood as an indictment against close relationships. As we mentioned in chapter 4, Bowen was not anticonnectedness. However, Bowen believed that the process of differentiation was a *prerequisite* for healthy connection.

But is this necessarily so? Cannot processes for healthy connectedness provide a firm foundation from which individuality may grow? John Bowlby (1969, 1988) thought so. Contra Bowen, Bowlby believed that a *process of healthy connectedness was a prerequisite for developing individuality.* Bowlby called this process of healthy connectedness "attachment." Bowlby proposed that our sense of trust, security, and safety is established in infancy through the bonds that are formed between infants and primary caregivers. Bowlby studied the degree to which mothers were *attuned* to their infants' physical and emotional needs and the degree to which mothers were *available* to meet those needs. Based on this research, Bowlby developed his theory of attachment. Securely attached infants had caregivers who provided *a secure base* from which infants explored the world and *a safe haven* to which infants returned when the world became frightening. These caretakers were appropriately attuned and available to these infants. Securely attached infants were able to encounter new situations without an overwhelming degree of anxiety. They were also able to let their caretakers comfort them and help them calm down when they were upset.

In contrast, insecurely attached infants did not experience this kind of parenting. Their caregivers were either not well attuned to their needs or not consistently available to meet those needs. These infants learned that you could not count on others to help you when the world becomes frightening. Their caretakers were *not* there when these children needed them. Insecurely attached babies anxiously sought out their primary caregivers and clung to them (*I need you. Where are you?*), or they dismissed them (*I may need you but I can't count on you to be there*).

Connecting to others is hardwired into us, that is, it is a part of how God created us (Cozolino, 2006; Seigel, 1999). The quality of the bond between mother and infant changes the brain chemistry in both of them so that mothers are wired to bond with their offspring, and in a process that loosely resembles uploading documents from one computer to another, infants "upload" information on how safe or dangerous the world is through their neuronal link with their primary caregivers. Goleman (2006) reports that when the adult brain seems to be on idle, in fact "the brain's default activity . . . seems to be mulling over our relationships" (p. 68). We are made to connect emotionally with one another across our life span.

Not surprising then is Bowlby's proposal that secure attachment is not just an appropriate need of infants; it is also a healthy need that continues into adulthood. According to attachment theory, it is normal for adults to desire close relationships with others who will be there when their world becomes frightening. From an attachment perspective, healthy relationships are characterized by *interdependency*—not self-sufficiency or emotional dependency. When we experience secure attachment as adults, the other to whom we are connected becomes *a safe haven and a secure base* for us.

If we have experienced secure attachment, we see ourselves as worthy and competent, and we see the world and others as relatively safe and trustworthy. Secure attachment or healthy connectedness helps us calm ourselves when we are in highly stressful situations. If we experienced insecure attachment, we see ourselves as unworthy, unlovable, or incompetent. We are never good enough. Other people are unreliable and untrustworthy, and the world is unsafe. Some individuals who experience insecure attachment desperately seek others upon whom they may cling. They long for closeness, but fear rejection. This is called anxious attachment. Other people who experience insecure attachment seem uninterested in developing close relationships. They try not to count on other people emotionally. This is called avoidant attachment. Notice how anxious attachment mirrors Bowen's idea of emotional fusion and how avoidant attachment reflects the Bowenian concept of emotional cutoff.

When people are securely attached, they can modulate their anxiety and appropriately manage their emotions during difficult interpersonal interactions. They have the skills to become a nonanxious presence. If people are anxiously attached, they tend to experience a heightened sense of distress when they experience relationship anxiety. They tend to pursue others to demand that differences are settled immediately. When people are avoidantly attached, they may say very little to the person with whom they are in conflict. They tend to withdraw when they are distressed (Wittenborn and Keiley, 2006). It seems as if the social centers of our brains are constantly deciding whether or not we like someone (Goleman, 2006).

When we discussed differentiation, we emphasized the importance of learning how to calm your self rather than relying on others to change to keep your anxiety level low. In contrast, attachment literature highlights the calming component of a *secure relationship*. Just as infants need adults to help them learn to self-soothe (Siegel, 1999), attachment theory proposes that *there are times* in our adult lives when the presence or even thought of key significant others can help us calm down. From an attachment perspective, emotional accessibility and responsiveness are key aspects of loving adult relationships. The important question from an attachment perspective is: *Will you be there when I need you?* Isolation and rejection (by someone who is important to us) are depressing and even traumatizing experiences, especially at strong moments of need. In our adult relationships, when we are injured by someone who we expected to be there for us during those painful or frightening times, we have experienced an injury to our sense of attachment with that person that we may frame as a substantial betrayal. As a side note, church leaders may have a parallel experience when they are injured by their denomination, which they had expected to be there for them.

Do congregations experience these kinds of attachment dynamics? Of course, they do! Church members bring their attachment expectations to church. Any pastor would love to have a church full of members with whom he or she is securely attached! These are individuals who make reasonable demands upon the pastor's time and attention, who are willing to serve in accordance with their gifts, and who can graciously tolerate the inevitable squabbles that arise when people work together for extended periods of time. But because the church is a place where broken people come to find healing, many who sit in the pews will attach to their pastor or church leader in anxious or avoidant ways. These are people who may make unreasonable and continuous demands on church leaders' time and attention, who may agree to serve only if their success is guaranteed or they may never agree to use their gifts at all. They may have a low tolerance for interpersonal tension. When persons are hurt by another church member to whom they have insecurely attached themselves, they may either leave the church without a word to anyone or they may complain bitterly to the church leader to whom they are the closest (think triangles).

Of course, church leaders also display secure and insecure attachment patterns. Any church would love to have a complement of secure church leaders. These are leaders who have reasonable expectations for their committee members, who can accept criticisms without falling apart or cutting others off, who can lead without coercion or manipulation, and who can offer support to others without getting support in return. Many with insecure attachment styles also stand in our pulpits and chair our committees. These are leaders who may need to be constantly affirmed and adored by others, who may lead through manipulation or control, who may not be able to take a stand when it is needed, or who may resign at the least sign of tension.

The good news is that attachment theory proposes that even though attachment styles are established in infancy, relationships with healthy adults can affect, *even change*, one's sense of attachment (Seigel, 1999). We think that the church could be a place where hurting people (i.e., those with insecure attachment experiences) can find a secure base and a safe haven for personal transformation. You can see how a vibrant relationship with Christ (spiritual maturity) is the securest base and the safest haven for challenging insecure attachment. Truly the Holy Spirit can transform hearts. Jesus' promise that "Lo, I am with you always" is a guarantee that those with even the most insecure of attachment styles can rely upon.

In addition, our membership in the body of Christ sets the stage for those who are more mature to come alongside those who need to mature. I (Toddy) watched this kind of transformation happen in the life of one pastor. Shortly after Pastor Morgan had begun his work in a new congregation, it came as a shock to both Pastor Morgan and the church leaders when intense and bitter conflict arose between them. Pastor Morgan experienced the leadership team as combative and uncooperative, unwilling to make the changes that Pastor Morgan suggested. Several key leaders experienced Pastor Morgan as controlling and dictatorial, unwilling to listen to their sound advice. Tensions continued to mount until Pastor Morgan despaired of his ability to remain in the ministry under these circumstances. He was on the verge of losing his soul for pastoring.

In the fullness of time, God blessed this pastor with several older, mature lay leaders who were willing to serve as mentors to Pastor Morgan, in effect providing the kind of safe haven and secure base for him to lead in. Transformation did not happen overnight. It took about three years. Pastor Morgan now leads the church from a more secure internal sense of self. This pastor is less anxious about others doing exactly what the pastor wants, is growing in the ability to delegate responsibility to others, and to not ride to the rescue if a delegated responsibility is not done perfectly. Ministry is now less about programs and progress and more about personal relationships with others who also want to grow in relational holiness.

What we want to highlight in this story is the key role that others played in the life of this man of God. Yes, Pastor Morgan did nurture a more differentiated self, did learn to self-soothe, and did learn to accept responsibility for misspoken words and leadership missteps, a process we highlighted in our chapter on emotional maturity. Yet Pastor Morgan did not go on a six-month silent retreat to a remote corner of the globe in order to experience these changes. *They happened in the context of his relationships with others.* There was no magical formula involved, there were no therapeutic tricks that turned the tide, there was no list of things that were done to "fix" the pastor. Instead there was the consistent presence of several key people who loved their pastor into maturity, who offered gentle rebuke when needed and genuine praise when appropriate. These others were *not trained mental health professionals!* They were brothers and sisters in Christ, who came alongside the pastor with a vision to help him grow spiritually, emotionally, and interpersonally. They were attuned and available to Pastor Morgan in a way that promoted greater security.

# Connectedness and Differentiation of Self

We propose that connectedness is an *essential aspect* of relational holiness, effective church leadership, and differentiation of self. Ronald Richardson (1996) expresses it like this:

> People at lower levels of emotional maturity often experience [individuality and closeness] as polar opposites, creating the sometimes "torn" experiences of life where we want to go in two directions at once. At this level, to be part of a group appears to mean that we have to sacrifice our individuality, and to be an individual appears to mean we have to sacrifice community.
>
> At higher levels of emotional maturity, we know more about how to keep these forces in balance within our lives, and we see situations less in terms of having to sacrifice either a part of ourselves or our connections

with others. It is possible to be a self and to be well connected to others, but "it ain't easy." (p. 57)

To illustrate the link between connectedness and differentiation of self, let us think in terms of our physical bodies. The individual cells in our body work best when each cell maintains its own cellular boundary while it is *closely and appropriately connected* to other cells. The cells must be connected *and* differentiated. In a similar way, Paul uses the metaphor of the physical body in 1 Corinthians 12 to discuss the church as the body of Christ. Paul writes:

> But in fact God has placed the parts in the body, every one of them, just as he wanted them to be. If they were all one part [i.e., undifferentiated or fused], where would the body be? As it is, there are many parts [differentiated individuality], but one body [connectedness]. The eye cannot say to the hand, "I don't need you!" And the head cannot say to the feet, "I don't need you!" [cutoff]. . . . Now you are the body of Christ [connectedness], and each one of you is a part of it [individuality]. (1 Cor. 12:18-21, 27 TNIV)

We believe that relational holiness requires both capacities—the capacity to maintain one's individuality without disconnecting and the capacity to experience closeness without emotional fusion. Shults and Sandage (2006) echo this perspective when they refer to mature spiritual development as "differentiated attachment." They write:

> Spiritual maturity in the Christian tradition can be described as a relational spirituality of *differentiated attachment.* . . . Theories of attachment and differentiation both suggest that maturity includes a willingness to explore, resilience in the midst of suffering, and a healthy sense of boundaries. These are all qualities of relational spiritual maturity. (p. 269)

Relational holiness as differentiated attachment should ideally begin with church leaders. If you think you struggle with this, what can you do? Taking into account what we have already said about differentiation of self and triangulation, and considering what we have just presented about attachment, we recommend the following practices (Entin, 1992; Wittenborn and Keiley, 2006).[1]

**Step 1: Become a master observer of yourself and the situation.**

Try to become a relationship anthropologist. Observe what you do when you become anxious. Listen to what you say and how you say things. Notice when your feelings begin to become aroused by attending to specific thoughts and sensations in your body. Attend to what you do when you have strong negative feelings. Watch what the other people say and do in response to you. Hear what they say and how they say it. What can you learn about yourself through these observations? Gaining insight means that you accept the pressures and admit the problems that exist in how others relate to you and how you relate to them. Observe how others react to you when under pressure. See what part *you may play* in keeping the stress going.

This type of self-exploration is not easy. Not one of us wakes up in the morning and says, "Today I want to act like a jerk when someone disagrees with me." Unfortunately, we may indeed be jerklike instead of Christlike when we lack self-awareness, because we tend to blame others for how we behave instead of holding ourselves accountable. When we lack insight, we tend to become very agitated when others offer us feedback about ourselves, even when that feedback is presented kindly and gently. If you find yourself defensively saying, "I'm not like that. I don't do that. If *you* hadn't . . . I wouldn't have . . ." when someone who *is trustworthy* offers you feedback, or if you get the same feedback from different people, then you may have blinders on. Just like Paul needed Ananias to help him following his Damascus Road encounter with Christ (Acts 9), those of us who cannot see ourselves need the help of a spiritual guide, a professional counselor, or a mentor.

Remember that the point is for you to allow the Holy Spirit to *change you, not fix other people.* It would be nice if you could wave a spiritual magic wand and change others, but you do not have that power. Only the Holy Spirit can change another's heart. However, by changing how *you* interact with someone—by not resorting to cutoff or fusion and by remaining relatively nonanxious—you automatically challenge the other to act differently. You can then trust the Holy Spirit to do what the Spirit does best.

**Step 2: Stop and find a space to calm yourself.**
Before you follow your typical knee-jerk reactions, stop and make a space within yourself to calm yourself down just long enough to think about what this powerful negative reaction is all about. The point is not to shut your feelings down or to act on them impulsively. The goal is to become aware of what you feel and what you can learn about yourself at this moment through these feelings. The objective is to be able to do this in the moment, that is, to calm yourself when you first realize that you are

growing more anxious and to reflect. The reality is that most of us will not be able to do this right away. We will realize that we have overreacted *in hindsight*. At this later moment in time, you can still think about what those powerful emotions told you about yourself. Spend some time in prayer. Bring the encounter before God and ask God to reveal the truth about yourself to you. Remind yourself that the Lord is with you always and will not abandon you during these trying times.

One of the "holy devices" the church has historically recommended to make space within ourselves, particularly in stressful moments, is to pray a breath prayer such as the Jesus prayer: *Lord Jesus Christ, Son of God, have mercy upon me, a sinner.* Such a prayer allows you to intentionally move your focal attention away from exclusively centering on the crisis at hand in order that you might refocus on the Lord Jesus Christ and all that he can do to bring his salvation and deliverance into the difficult setting. This crucial shift of attention allows the Lord to help you rein in anxiety while opening your heart in faith, hope, and love to the goodness of God.

**Step 3: Identify your underlying feelings.**

Our anxiety is often triggered by fear of abandonment or fear of absorption. Which fear has been activated in this situation with these people? Other additional feelings may be in play as well. For example, you may also be feeling sad, hurt, or embarrassed. These feelings often hide underneath anger. Anger pushes others away while these more vulnerable feelings help us connect. Is this a time to share your more vulnerable side or not? Pray for wisdom and greater insight into your own heart: *Lord Jesus, help me not allow the weapons of darkness, such as anxiety, fear, and malice, to take root in my heart. Give me courage, instead, to depend upon your sweet presence to fill me with the fruit of your Spirit.*

**Step 4: Lower your anxiety by taking charge of yourself.**

Do you need to take a few calming breaths? Are you talking to yourself in ways that will keep you anxious or that will calm you down? Have you let your emotional brain hijack your thinking brain? What do you need to do to get your thinking brain back in control? Try slowing things down. Pay attention to how fast you are talking or how loud you are getting. If you are talking too fast or too loudly because you are anxious, push the pause button. This process is not about being passionless. It is, however, about not letting yourself get out of hand! It is about being in control of your words and actions. For example, I (Toddy) was attending a board meeting where one board member was becoming highly irritated with others on the board. At one point she said, "I am getting too loud.

Let me calm down." She took a deep breath. Then, without skipping a beat, this woman lowered her voice, slowed the rate of her speech, and continued to make her point with passion. I noticed that we all took her internal change as a cue to check our own pulse rate.

**Step 5: Take the other's perspective without taking responsibility for him or her.**

Listen carefully to the other person and clarify your understanding of his or her thoughts and feelings. Often this means that you have to stop planning what you are going to say next so that you can fully attend to what the other person is saying. Try to imagine what fears may be triggering that person's anxiety. Check out your interpretation with the speaker and believe the speaker if he or she corrects your perception. Taking another's perspective does not mean that you give up your own beliefs about an issue. Once your conversation partner knows that you understand his or her position, this person is in a better place to listen to you. Clearly communicate your own point of view when you do speak. You do not need to control, manipulate, or withdraw. Be careful to not over function, that is, do not comply just to get the other person off your back. Also, be prepared to say no if that is appropriate given your context. Moreover, be ready to cooperate if your conversation partner's perspective makes sense to you and does make a difference in how you view the overall situation. This is not losing face. This is acting maturely.

**Step 6: Remain in control of yourself.**

As you diminish your anxiety and emotional reactivity, you will be able to *think* about the stress and develop alternative ways to manage the situation. When we are emotionally reactive we have a tendency to demand that others comply and conform. We experience differences as threats. When you remain in control of yourself, you are freer to imagine other possible ways to solve problems and you are less likely to view the other person as your enemy. Saint Paul instructed his younger protégé, Timothy, to "guard the good treasure" (2 Tim 1:14) that had been entrusted to him. In like manner, we are called to guard our hearts against the intrusion of faithless reactivity.

*The goal of remaining in control is to protect the relationship from damage that may be irreparable.* We all know that the children's rhyme "sticks and stones may break my bones but words will never hurt me" is a lie. Perhaps this is why the biblical writers attended carefully to how we speak to one another. Proverbs is full of advice about wise and foolish speech and James declared that the tongue is "a restless evil, full of deadly poison. . . .

Out of the same mouth come praise and cursing" (James 3:8, 10 NIV). Church leaders in particular must remain in control of their tongues as they have the ability to wound many people, and, likewise, church leaders should develop thicker skin (i.e., differentiation of self) so that they are not undone by the misspoken words of those with whom they work. This will be easier for those leaders who come to their task with a sense of secure attachment. Church leaders who may have an insecure relationship with specific others in the congregation may need the support of a spiritual mentor, a professional counselor, or a mature friend to help them sort through their distressing emotions when they feel like they are being verbally attacked.

Sometimes remaining in control requires that you call a time-out. You may want to exercise this option when you realize that you and your discussion partner are on the verge of losing emotional control of the argument. Characteristics of a good time-out include: identifying the need for the time out, recommending the amount of time desired, and naming the time when you will return to the conversation. While you are in time-out, your focus should be on calming and quieting yourself, not on marshalling your next round of arguments and not on mentally rehearsing the previous conversation in ways that keep you emotionally aroused.

The advent of email has made taking an *electronic* time-out very important. It is too easy for church leaders to write their anger or disappointment in an email and then send it without taking the time to consider how the message will impact the recipient. While you may be fortunate enough to "unsend" a hostile message before it has been opened, you cannot count on that! Better to not have sent it at all than to pour electronic salt on an open emotional wound through your e-note. Our advice is that the kind of conversations that are likely to make people highly anxious are best handled face-to-face, where you have the benefit of facial expressions, body language, and immediate feedback to help you interpret the other person's perspective.

**Step 7: Consider expressing your underlying feelings.**

*If the situation is appropriate,* you may risk expressing your more vulnerable feelings (fear, loss, sadness, embarrassment, and so on) with the other person. You might also express your best guess about what the other person's underlying, more vulnerable feelings are, but this part is not necessary. With this step you have shifted the discussion from talk about the content of your disagreement to talk about your emotional process. Vulnerable feelings allow connection, but the fear of taking this risk often gets in the way.

For example, I (Toddy) was talking with a supervisor about a responsibility that I wanted to take on but my supervisor disagreed with my proposal. I felt strongly about this and so did the supervisor. I could sense my anxiety rising. I could sense that she might be interpreting my persistence as a challenge to her authority. I had only recently come under her supervision and this was the first encounter where I challenged her on an issue. I can imagine that she felt as if she had a lot at stake as I continued to press the issue.

I did not want to damage my relationship with this supervisor, nor did I want to cave in. I took a breath to steady myself. Instead of explaining why I felt I was capable of handling this responsibility, I shifted from a discussion of the content (what we were talking about) to a comment about *how* this conversation was affecting our relationship (a discussion of our process). I said, "I really didn't intend this conversation to become a power struggle between us, and I don't want to jeopardize our working relationship." I wasn't using the classic formula of "I feel ____ about this" as a way to share my underlying emotions, but my words communicated that message nevertheless. The tone of the discussion changed immediately. We both calmed down. She affirmed her desire to have a good working relationship with me and her respect for my judgment. However, you need to know that I adhered to my supervisor's decision. I did not get my way! Nevertheless, we developed a stronger working relationship because of how we managed this discussion.

In contrast, an underlying issue that I (Steve) have seen in far too many spiritual leaders' lives is an outright unwillingness to live under the authority of another. When we write about expressing our feelings, we need to be honest enough to also express some of our deepest drives to have our own way regardless of the cost. Ask yourself the question, "Do I always have to be right about everything?" If the answer is yes, then a wonderful dose of humility in the Lord is far overdue. The truth is that none of us always see the whole picture of any given situation. The safeguard in Scripture for us is the call to respect those in authority over us and to live under their judgments.

**Step 8: Connect.**

When we manage our anxiety well enough, are clear about our position, and respectful of the other person and their position, we preserve our connection with one another. This becomes a solid platform for future discussions and better decisions. Taking time to reconnect may take the form of calling a moratorium on the contended topic of conversation.

During this time we can seek God's guidance and ask others for their input. You may even have a conversation about your conversation. You can talk together about what made the discussion difficult and what made the discussion go well, what you need to change when you begin talking about the topic, and what safeguards you need to keep in place.

# Relational Ethics in the Church Family

In a previous section we used the lens of attachment to describe what righteous relationships might look like. From this viewpoint, church members become a safe haven and a secure base for one another. A second lens that we can use to describe righteous relationships is what attends to the ways in which love and trust are manifested within the church. From this relational perspective *trust means that I can give freely to you knowing that at some point I can count on you to give to me what I need.* This definition of trust implies a history of mutual and reliable giving and receiving (Boszormenyi-Nagy and Krasner, 1986; Hargrave, 2000).

Establishing loving and trustworthy relationships begins with the leaders of any group. For example, in loving and trustworthy families, parents take care of the physical and emotional needs of children in predictable and appropriate ways. Minimally this means that children can trust their parents to provide food, clothing, shelter, and nurture. In unloving and untrustworthy families, parents cannot be depended upon to provide the physical or emotional safety and security that children need to grow, that is, parents are neglectful or abusive. Over the long-term, this inverse of giving and receiving, of blessing and burden, results in something called destructive entitlement (Boszormenyi-Nagy and Krasner, 1986). Destructive entitlement means that formerly abused or neglected children may enter adulthood with an attitude that declares either "now it's my turn to get what I was denied as a child" or their attitude may declare "my role in life is to take care of you because I do not deserve to be given due consideration."

When church leaders connect with church members in loving and trustworthy ways, the entire body may grow in relational holiness. However, when church leaders connect with church members in ways that are unloving and untrustworthy, that is, when leaders take more than they give, when they gather more benefits than is their fair share, church leaders or members may experience a form of destructive entitlement. In the church this may mean that one does not name the sinful behavior in which their leaders are engaged but instead joins with the church leader to blame the victim for the leader's downfall. Such is often the case when clergy violate sexual boundaries. The "other woman" is often accused of causing the leader to fall into sin, as though the church leader had no obligation or power to maintain his personal and professional boundaries.[2]

Consider for a moment how antithetical these dysfunctional ways of connecting are to the Wesleyan call to relational holiness. Church leaders who embody these unrighteous ways of relating to others have an outward form of godliness, but they do not let the convicting power of the Holy Spirit call them to accountability. They may indeed feel guilt and shame for their untrustworthy and unloving actions, but rather than repent and seek forgiveness, they keep their sin a secret. By doing so they allow themselves opportunities to continue to sin against God and against others. Their anxiety about getting caught is greater than their desire to develop holy habits. In some strange way they gain a sense of identity, a sense of self, from their sin, rather than securing their sense of self in their relationship with Christ.

Interrupting these patterns of unholy relationships requires the power of the Spirit, a commitment to the well-being of those who are being confronted, and a deep concern for those who have been victimized by a misuse of power. This means that those who are confronting such relational unrighteousness must view others through the eyes of Christ. They can relate to offenders with a firmness that is peppered with love and compassion. They should also have a desire to see the wounded ones restored to wholeness. These attitudes require nothing short of fasting and prayer! It also requires the strength of differentiation of self. Such situations generate anxiety within even the most emotionally mature believers. There is no way around that! One confronts others best from a position of differentiation and maturity in the Lord.

This relational perspective on love and trust recognizes that many relationships exist in which there is an imbalance of giving and receiving, of obligations and entitlement. There will surely be times when some give more while others receive more. We might argue that this is *always* the case in our relationship with God! "For God so loved the world that he gave his one and only Son, that whoever believes in him shall not perish but have eternal life" (John 3:16 NIV). God's ability to give far outstrips our ability to give back. In fact, God's capacity to give to us is also *infinitely greater than our capacity to receive from God.* We relate to God in an asymmetrical way. God has the greater capacity for personal relatedness, and God, in effect, carries our relationship because God accepts what we can return to him.[3]

This is the case with parenting. The giving and receiving between parents and children is asymmetrical, so that parents give far more than they receive from their children. *This is also true for many church leadership positions.* Church leaders regularly give more than they may receive back. Any pastor knows this reality quite well! Church leaders who are nurturing relational holiness intuitively recognize this reality and are able to seek support for themselves so that they can continue to give to the church in appropriate ways. Church members also recognize this reality. Those church members who are nurturing relational holiness will find ways to recognize the contribution that church leaders make to the life of the church. In this way a balance between giving and receiving is maintained.

# Conclusion

Noted theologian G. K. Chesterton (1927) wrote: "There comes an hour in the afternoon when the child is tired of 'pretending'; when he is weary of being a robber. . . . It is then that he torments the cat" (p. 187). I (Toddy) have reflected on that quotation often, in part because of my sympathies with the poor cat, and in part because of my empathy with church leaders who struggle to maintain a passion for the ministries to which God has called them. Phrased another way, Chesterton's quote could read like so: Late in the afternoon, when church leaders tire of pretending, when they are weary of being pastors, chair persons, lay leaders, youth workers, and so on—that's when they can very easily end up tormenting their congregations with their own personal deformities. Church leaders can end up tormenting their congregation by being pastoral dictators or just the opposite, pastoral cowards. We can wound others by being more powerful (taking over) or by abdicating the responsibilities that are rightfully ours to assume (under responsibility). If we restate the issue with an emphasis on *solution* rather than *problem*, it could read like this: *What will keep church leaders fresh late in the afternoon so that their heart for ministry remains vibrant through the entire day?*[4]

That is the question that we have sought to answer. By now you know that we think that relational holiness is vitally important to staying fresh in the ministry—to saving your soul, to use the metaphor with which we began. In previous chapters we have proposed that church leaders with deepening levels of relational holiness are those whose identities are rooted and grounded in a vibrant and growing relationship with Christ. Based on the security of their relationship with Christ, such leaders also have vibrant and growing relationships with others. They are comfortable working closely with others in the church and they are capable of acting independently. Furthermore, we have explained how unchecked relationship anxiety sabotages church leaders as it elicits knee-jerk reactions instead of thoughtful responses. We have explored how spiritual, emotional, and interpersonal maturity not only promote growth in relational holiness, they also provide an antidote to this type of anxiety. We have suggested that this enables church leaders to embody personal and social holiness in the midst of difficult interpersonal relationships.

Church leaders can return to the safety and security of the Father's loving arms during times of high anxiety. In the embrace of the Father, church leaders will hear the whispered, "Peace. I am with you always." As leaders recall how God has acted redemptively on their behalf in the past, they will be able to access the Holy Spirit to calm their hearts and to relieve their troubled minds. While Scripture challenges us to go on to maturity (Heb 6), we nevertheless remain children in our relationship with God. God forever remains the safe haven into which believers retreat when the world presses in and the secure base from which believers go out into the world for the sake of the wounded and the lost.

Church leaders can courageously begin to master their own emotional reactivity. Recall that this is a way of nonanxiety and self-responsibility. It begins by becoming curious about how you contribute to the relationship dilemmas you face, rather than exclusively blaming others for them. You then adopt a researcher stance to objectively observe how you function within the context of your relationships. You subsequently develop ways to calm yourself down when you begin to become reactive so that you can think more clearly, more neutrally, and more objectively about the situation. Finally, you learn how to remain emotionally present in the midst of anxious others. In these ways you can lead your church without losing your soul.

# NOTES

## 1. It's Not about Me . . . or Is It?

1. Theologians Tom Oord and Michael Lodahl also use this term in their book by the same title, *Relational Holiness* (Kansas City, Mo.: Beacon Hill Press, 2005).

2. Steve Sandage has recently proposed a heuristic model of relational spirituality that includes one's relationship with God, self, and others. For Steve's discussion of his model, we refer you to F. LeRon Shults and Steven J. Sandage, *Transforming Spirituality* (Grand Rapids: Baker Publishing House, 2006), 221.

3. See the first English woman of letters, Julian of Norwich (1978), who wrote, "God wants us to pay attention to his words, and always to be strong in our certainty, in well-being and in woe, for he loves us and delights in us, and so he wishes us to love him and delight in him and trust greatly in him, and all will be well" (p. 165).

4. Social psychology can describe this phenomenon as the fundamental attribution error wherein I attribute the good things I experience as a result of my character and the troubles I experience as the result of circumstances that surround me, which can often be framed as reasons for my responding as I did. On the other hand, I attribute the good things that you experience as a result of external circumstances (what do you want now?) and the bad things that you experience as a result of your flawed character (it's just like you to ____).

## 2. Anxiety: The Gift That Keeps on Giving

1. Murray Bowen does not use the term *togetherness* in the same way that John Bowlby used the term *attachment*. For those who are into attachment theory, you can loosely associate the force of togetherness with insecure attachment. We explore the link between attachment theory and relational holiness in chapter 6.

2. It is also true that over-responsible lay church leaders may pair up with under-responsible ordained clergy.

## 4. Relational Holiness: Emotional Maturity

1. Drs. Henry Cloud and John Townsend have written extensively on boundaries within a Christian framework. For information on their books and resources, go to www.cloudtownsend.com.

2. This vignette represents no actual person. Instead, it is a composite from stories that are found in Virginia T. Holeman, *Reconcilable Differences: Hope and Healing for Troubled Marriages* (Downers Grove, Ill.: InterVarsity Press, 2004).

3. We affirm that clergy affairs are nothing less than abuse of power and trust. The pastor holds the position of power, and whether or not the pastor feels empowered, the pastor is solely responsible for his or her actions and reactions. Clergy affairs wreak havoc on the pastor's family, the family of the affairee, the local church, and beyond. For a more complete discussion of clergy sexual misconduct, we refer you to Stanley Grenz and R. Bell, *Betrayal of Trust: Sexual Misconduct in the Pastorate* (Downers Grove, Ill.: InterVarsity Press, 1995).

4. For example, The United Methodist Church has identified skilled persons to serve as advocates for individuals who have been wounded by clergy sexual abuse.

5. Portions of this chapter are based on Holeman, *Reconcilable Differences: Hope and Healing for Troubled Marriages*.

6. This could include meeting in a public setting like a restaurant or meeting at the church at times when others are in the building and near the meeting room. This offers a degree of safety for both pastor and parishioner.

## 5. Relational Holiness: Interpersonal Maturity

1. We also recommended that the hardest, but most "growthful" way through gridlock is to go on to maturity through a process of differentiation of self.

2. Counseling sessions are a unique setting where trained pastoral or professional counselors use the principles of triangulation to create what is called a "therapeutic triangle." Here the counselor intentionally inserts himself or herself into the relationship turmoil and acts as a thermostat to help people manage their anxiety. If this is of interest to you, you will find help in Philip Guerin's book *Working with Relationship Triangles*. And even the most skilled therapists wind up in nontherapeutic triangles from time to time!

3. Our suggestion at this point is for the parents to move closer to the beau by getting to know him, inviting him to dinner, and so on. This is no guarantee that the daughter will move away from the beau, but it is a more likely outcome than if the parents reactively challenge her. The parents could also *calmly* ask the daughter to think about the relationship she has with her beau. The pivotal point for the parents is to stay calm during the discussion.

## 6. Relational Holiness and Righteous Relationships

1. A. K. Wittenborn, and M. K. Keiley, *Multiple couple group intervention: A new approach to premarital counseling.* Paper presented at the meeting of the American Association for Marriage and Family Therapy, Austin, Texas, 2006. Used by permission.

2. We recognize that women are also capable of sexual misconduct in the pastorate. However, men are currently in the overwhelming majority of those pastors who are guilty of clergy sexual misconduct and abuse. That is why we choose to use male pronouns.

3. Regarding asymmetric relatedness, Warren Brown (Hardy, 2001) notes that "one person with greater relational capacity can uphold and sustain relationalness . . . of another person. I think we stand that way in relationship to God. We're all in some ways

autistic in the sense that God is extending to us asymmetrically a relatedness that we only barely reciprocate. So, in that sense—in any absolute sense—our differences in abilities or capacities are not nearly as critical as the fact that God is extending to us and relating" (p. 24).

4. I first heard the idea of staying "fresh late in the afternoon" in a keynote address by Dr. Earl Palmer decades ago (ca. 1980) at a National Youth Workers Convention in Detroit, Michigan.

# REFERENCES

Allender, D. B. 2006. *Leading with a limp*. Colorado Springs, Colo.: Waterbrook Press.

Augustine. 1960. *The confessions of St. Augustine*. Trans. J. K. Ryan. Garden City, N.Y.: Image Books.

Boszormenyi-Nagy, I. and B. R. Krasner. 1986. *Between give and take: A clinical guide to contextual therapy*. New York: Brunner/Mazel.

Bowlby, J. 1969. *Attachment*. Vol. 1 of *Attachment and loss*. New York: Basic Books.

———. 1988. *A secure base: Clinical applications of attachment theory*. New York: Basic Books.

Campbell, T. A. and M. T. Burns. 2004. *Wesleyan essentials in a multi-cultural society*. Nashville: Abingdon Press.

Chesterton, G. K. 1927. *The everlasting man*. London: Hodder and Stoughton.

Collins, K. 2007. *The theology of John Wesley: Holy love and the shape of grace*. Nashville: Abingdon Press.

Cozolino, L. 2006. *The neuroscience of human relationships: Attachment and the developing social brain*. New York: W. W. Norton & Company.

Entin, A. D. 1992. A family systems approach to the healthy family. *Topics in Family Psychology & Counseling* 1:53-61.

Friedman, Edwin H. 1985. *Generation to generation: Family process in church and synagogue*. New York: Guilford Press.

Gilbert, R. M. 1992. *Extraordinary relationships: A new way of thinking about human interactions*. Minneapolis: Chronimed Publishing.

Gingrich, F. 2004. Attachment or differentiation-of-self: Competing or complementary theoretical orientations in contemporary relational therapies. *Marriage and family: a Christian journal* 7:33-49.

Goleman, D. 1995. *Emotional intelligence*. New York: Bantam Books.

————. 2006. *Social intelligence: The new science of human relationships*. New York: Bantam Books.

Gottman, J. M. and N. Silver. 1999. *The seven principles for making marriage work*. New York: Crown.

Green, J. B. 1997. *The gospel of Luke*. New International Commentary on the New Testament. Grand Rapids: Wm. B. Eerdmans Publishing.

Gregory of Nyssa. 1978. *The life of Moses*. Trans. A. Malherbe and E. Ferguson. New York: Paulist Press.

————. 1979. *From glory to glory: Texts from Gregory of Nyssa's mystical writings*. Trans. H. Musurillo. Crestwood, N.Y.: St. Vladimir's Seminary Press.

Grenz, S. J. 2001. *The social God and the relational self: A Trinitarian theology of the imago Dei*. Louisville, Ky.: Westminster John Knox Press.

Grenz, S. and R. Bell. 1995. *Betrayal of trust: Sexual misconduct in the pastorate*. Downers Grove, Ill.: InterVarsity Press.

Guerin, Philip J., Jr, Thomas F. Fogarty, Leo F. Fay, and Judith Gilbert Kautto. 1996. *Working with relationship triangles: The one-two-three of psychotherapy*. New York: Guilford Press.

Hardy, D. 2001. Theologians of a kind: Trinity Church Conference speakers on what it is to be human. *Research News & Opportunities in Science and Theology* 2:24-25.

Hargrave, T. 2000. *The essential humility of marriage: Honoring the third identity in couple therapy*. Phoenix: Zeig, Tucker, & Theisen.

Harper, S. 1995. *Devotional life in the Wesleyan tradition: A workbook*. Nashville: Upper Room Books.

Headley, A. J. 1999. *Achieving balance in ministry*. Kansas City, Mo.: Beacon Hill Press.

Holeman, V. T. 2004. *Reconcilable differences: Hope and healing for troubled marriages*. Downers Grove, Ill.: InterVarsity Press.

Howatch, S. 1987. *Glittering images*. New York: Fawcett Columbine.

Julian of Norwich. 1978. *Showings*. Trans. E. Colledge and J. Walsh. New York: Paulist Press.

Kerr, M. and M. Bowen. 1988. *Family evaluation: An approach based on Bowen theory*. New York: W. W. Norton & Company.

Klever, P. 2003. Marital functioning and multigenerational cutoff. In *Emotional cutoff: Bowen family systems theory perspectives*, ed. P. Titelman, 219-43. New York: The Haworth Clinical Practice Press.

Maddox, R. L. 1994. *Responsible grace: John Wesley's practical theology*. Nashville: Abingdon Press.

Moltmann, J. 1981. *God in creation: A new theology of creation and the spirit of God.* Trans. Margaret Kohl. San Francisco: Harper & Row.

Muto, S. and A. van Kaam. 2005. *Growing through the stress of ministry.* Totowa, N.J.: Resurrection Press.

Northumbria Community. 2002. *Celtic daily prayers: Prayers and readings from the Northumbria Community.* San Francisco: Harper SanFrancisco.

Pannenberg, W. 1991. *Systematic theology,* vol. 1. Trans. G. W. Bromily. Grand Rapids: Wm. B. Eerdmans Publishing.

Richardson, R. W. 1996. *Creating a healthier church: Family systems theory, leadership, and congregational life.* Minneapolis: Fortress Press.

———. (2005). *Becoming a healthier pastor: Family systems theory and the pastor's own family.* Minneapolis: Fortress Press.

Scazzero, P. 2003. *The emotionally healthy church.* Grand Rapids: Zondervan.

Schnarch, D. 1997. *Passionate marriage.* New York: W. W. Norton & Company.

———. 2002. *Resurrecting sex.* New York: HarperCollins.

Seamands, S. 2005. *Ministry in the image of God: The Trinitarian shape of Christian service.* Downers Grove, Ill.: InterVarsity Press.

Seigel, D. J. 1999. *The developing mind: How relationships and the brain interact to shape who we are.* New York: Guilford Press.

Shults, F. L. and S. J. Sandage. 2006. *Transforming spirituality: Integrating theology and psychology.* Grand Rapids: Baker Academic.

Smith, W. H., Jr. 2003. Emotional cutoff and family stability: Child abuse in family emotional process. In *Emotional cutoff: Bowen family systems theory perspectives,* ed. P. Titelman, 351-75. New York: The Haworth Clinical Practice Press.

Steinke, P. L. 1993. *How your church family works: Understanding congregations as emotional systems.* Washington, D.C.: The Alban Institute.

———. 1996. *Healthy congregations: A systems approach.* Washington, D.C.: The Alban Institute.

Titelman, Peter. 2003. Emotional cutoff in Bowen family systems theory: An overview. In *Emotional cutoff: Bowen family systems theory perspectives,* ed. P. Titelman, 9-66. New York: The Haworth Clinical Practice Press.

Van Kaam, A. and S. Muto. 2004. *Foundations of Christian formation.* Vol. 1 of *Formation theology.* Pittsburgh: Epiphany Association.

———. 2005. *Christian articulation of the mystery.* Vol. 2 of *Formation theology.* Pittsburgh: Epiphany Association.

————. 2006. *Formation of the Christian heart.* Vol. 3 of *Formation theology.* Pittsburgh: Epiphany Association.

Wesley, John. 1966. *A plain account of Christian perfection.* Kansas City, Mo.: Beacon Hill Press.

White, J., and H. D. Center. 2002. Influencing change in Bowenian differentiation of self through Cloud and Townsend's boundaries instruction. *Marriage and family: A Christian journal* 5:525-37.

Willard, D. 1998. *The divine conspiracy: Rediscovering our hidden life in God.* San Francisco: HarperSanFrancisco.

Wittenborn, A. K. and B. K. Keiley. 2006. *Multiple couple group intervention: A new approach to premarital counseling.* Paper presented at the meeting of the American Association for Marriage and Family Therapy, Austin, Texas.

Young, C. 1989. Confession and Pardon. In *The United Methodist hymnal,* 12. Nashville: The United Methodist Publishing House.

# INDEX